Lean and Green Diet Cookbook 2021

550+ Satisfying & Healthy Lean and Green Recipes to Improve Your Wellness and Quick Weight Loss

Wendy McFarlane

Table of Contents

Introduction

Lean and Green diet is a popular meal replacement program that participants have confirmed is very useful in rapid weight loss. The diet is observed by combining "Fuelings" (such as bars, shakes, and many other pre-packaged foods) with a six-small-meals-per-day principle to help people lose weight without going through strenuous exercises but consuming calories in a minimal amount throughout the day.

There is also provision for a health coach that the consumer can relate with, and he or she will guide the consumer while taking the diet program and will give support, motivation, and encouragement.

Several "Lean and Green" recipes you will be eating while taking the program are also provided, and with this, you can enjoy the best of this diet program.

Lean and Green diet enhances weight loss through branded products known as "Fuelings" while the homemade entrées are referred to as the "Lean and Green" meals. The Fuelings are made up of over 60 items, specifically low in carbs (carbohydrates) but high in probiotic cultures and protein. The fuelings ultimately contain friendly bacteria that can help boost gut health. They include cookies, bars, puddings, shakes, soups, cereals, and pasta.

Looking at the listed foods, you might think they are relatively high in carbs, which is understandable, but the Fuelings are composed so that they are lower in sugar and carbs than the traditional versions of similar foods.

The company does this by using small-portion sizes and sugar substitutes. Many of the Fuelings are packed with soy protein isolate and whey protein powder in furtherance. Those who are interested in the Lean and Green diet plan but are not interested in cooking or have no chance for it are provided with pre-made, low-carb meals. These meals are referred to as "Flavors of Home," and they can sufficiently replace the Lean and Green Meals.

The company explicitly states that by working with its team of coaches and following the Lean and Green diet as required, you will achieve a "lifelong transformation, one healthy habit at a time."

Therefore, to record success with this diet plan, you have to stick to the Fuelings supplemented by veggie, meat, and healthy fat entrée daily; you will be full and nourished. Although you will be consuming low calories, you will not be losing a lot of muscle since you will be feeding on lots of fiber, protein, and other vital nutrients. Your calories as an adult will not exceed 800–1,000. You can lose 12 pounds in 12 weeks if you follow the 5&1 Optimal Weight Plan option.

Since you will curb your carb intake while on this diet plan, you will naturally shed fat because the carb is the primary source of energy, therefore, if it is not readily available, the body finds a fat alternative, which implies that the body will have to break down your fats for energy and keep burning fat.

Finally, with this book, you will determine if the Lean and Green diet program is a weight loss program convenient for you before you get started.

"I'm on a diet. I can't come for the weekend!" Punctually said Martha, a friend I have known since adolescence. She was always struggling with weight; she never saw herself right, and when we went out with the others, she had constant difficulties in choosing fashionable clothes like all of us. In reality, he didn't have that many kg in excess...maybe 5–6...? But this caused her low self-esteem and insecurity in any social context. After 27 years of diets, she got married and had a beautiful baby. Martha, during pregnancy, gained 30 kilograms! So that suffering resurfaces for her appearance, for the joint pains that lead her not to sleep at night, lethargy, and that sense of discomfort with her husband who saw her only with those XXL clothes. She was tired of diets that started on Monday and stopped for the weekend. She needed a fast, definitive, serious path, but above all, a support that would help her manage meals because now, with a family, she couldn't stop cooking and isolate herself.

So she knew the Lean and Green Diet, a low-carb path with a high-protein content, and is immediately struck because it was based on a choice of over 60 healthy and fast solutions, including shakes, bars, soups, biscuits, salty snacks ... high content protein, with probiotics and prebiotics to promote correct absorption of nutrients and good digestion. In this way, she no longer had to waste time and money in supermarkets, looking for refined and unavailable ingredients!!

She could choose between 3 different routes that would bring her to a healthy weight. Martha chose the strongest and fastest 5&1, moving on to 4&2&1 and then to 3&3. It is a path that is not based only on substitute meals but also on cooked meals, precisely to not become slaves to a product and learn to eat while losing weight healthily, not affecting lean mass. After a short time, her appearance began to change, not only for the loss of weight and size, but for that radiant light on her face, different energy, and for the first time I saw her sitting at the table serene, without having to give up her social life. This book is for all those women who often step aside, at the expense of their happiness, but who deserve a new chance.

Martha finally found her solution with the Lean and Green diet, eliminating those 30 kgs in a few months and entering the size 40 she had always sought. To date, after two years, it has never started again, dispelling the myth that by following low-calorie routes, one gains weight quickly. First of all, because with this diet you eat 6 times a day and the kg you recover is determined exclusively by the incorrect lifestyle, you are applying at that moment and not by the previous one. This book also serves as mental support on approaching a definitive path of transformation and is perhaps my favorite part because it is essential to keep in mind why you started and where you want to go. I believe that each of us deserves to feel better, feel full of energy, and not underestimate ourselves as a woman!!

And since we women like to share our secrets, here you can find many: on how not to finally give up on social life, how to organize yourself with meals, how to meet the needs of the whole family, how to find yourself without guilt and many healthy, practical and tasty recipes that will lead you to be satisfied even in the kitchen, regaining your physical shape, and without having to count calories anymore! You will have a list of foods to prefer and avoid that you can always carry with you and some practical tricks on smart shopping! We will start with the first action: cleaning the kitchen pantries of all those pre-packaged foods, which intoxicate us, make room for healthy foods, and combine them in a conscious, stimulating, and fun way! And then, let's face it: the healthier you eat, the more your body will ask for healthy things! Enjoy this book and your wellness journey with the Lean and Green diet!

What is Lean and Green Diet

Lean and Green is basically a weight loss or weight maintenance program that suggests the use of a lean and green meal along with processed food called "fueling." The name Lean and Green for this diet originally came from the fueling brand Lean and Green which was launched by Medifast. And here is the concept of fueling is organized around the whole Lean and Green diet:

The diet says to add nutritional Fuelings to the diet while controlling the overall caloric intake.

The fueling is actually powdered food, which is mixed with liquid like water and then added to the diet as a part of routine meals.

Besides consuming these fueling, the dieters are also suggested to exercise 30 minutes daily to lose their weight.

By trying fueling as a substitute for real food, you can curb the carb and sugar intake and can manage your caloric intake as well.

How much Fuelings to consume, how much food to eat, and what to eat on this dietary regime depends on the type of weight loss plan you are going for. However, on this diet, the overall calorie intake for adults is reduced to 800 to 1000 per day, which lets you lose about 12 lbs of weight per 12 weeks on average.

It is worth noticing here that the Lean and Green diet also provides different methods of managing the Fuelings and lean and green meals during the day. There are three different plans that a person can opt according to his own preference and lifestyle to introduce Fuelings into his diet. The three Lean and Green diet plans include:

5 & 1 Plan: Five Fuelings and one lean and green meal a day

4, 2 & 1 Plan: Four Fuelings, two lean and green meal a day, and one snack

Weight-loss Benefits of Lean and Green Diet

The Lean and Green diet plan has some guidelines—especially in food consumption—that must be adhered to if you wish to record a diet plan successfully.

Foods That Are Not Allowed

Apart from the carbs contained in the pre-packaged Lean and Green fuelings, most carb-containing beverages and foods are not allowed while you are on the 5&1 plan.

Some fats are also banned as well as all fried foods.

Below are the foods you must avoid, except if they are included in your Fuelings:

Refined Grains: Pasta, pancakes, crackers, cookies, pastries, white bread, biscuits, flour tortillas, white rice, and cakes

Fried Foods: Fish, vegetables, shellfish, meats, and sweets like pastries

Whole Fat Dairy: Cheese, milk, and yogurt

Certain Fats: Coconut oil, butter, and solid shortening

Sugar-Sweetened Beverages: fruit juice, soda, energy drinks, sports drinks, and sweet tea

Alcohol: All varieties

The foods below are banned while on the 5&1 plan but are added to the 6-week transition phase and with no restriction during the 3&3 plan:

Fruits: All fresh fruits

Whole Grains: High-fibre breakfast cereal, whole grain bread, whole-wheat pasta, and brown rice

Starch Vegetables: Corn, white potatoes, sweet potatoes, and peas

Low-Fat or Fat-Free Dairy: Milk, yogurt, and cheese

Legumes: Beans, peas, lentils, and soybeans

Note that during the 6-week transition phase, and while on the 3&3 plan, you are advised to eat more berries if you must take fruits as they contain lower carbs.

Recommended Foods to Eat

The foods you are liable to eat while on the 5&1 plan are the 5 Lean and Green Fuelings and 1 Lean and Green meal daily.

The meals consist mainly of healthy fats, lean protein, and low-carb vegetables, and there is a recommendation for only two servings of fatty fish every week. Some beverages and low-carb condiments are also allowed in small proportions.

The Foods that Are allowed for the Lean and Green Meals

Fish and Shellfish: Trout, tuna, halibut, salmon, crab, scallops, lobster, and shrimp

Meat: Lean beef, lamb, chicken, game meats, turkey, tenderloin or pork chop, and ground meat (must be 8 5% lean at least)

Vegetable Oils: Walnut, flaxseed, olive oil, and canola

Eggs: Whole Eggs, egg beaters, and egg whites

Additional Healthy Fats: Reduced-fat margarine, walnuts, pistachios, almonds, avocado, olives, and low carb salad dressings

Soy Products: Tofu

Sugar-free Beverages: Unsweetened almond milk, coffee, tea, and water

Sugar-free Snacks: Gelatin, mints, popsicles, and gum

Low-Carb Vegetables: Celery, mushrooms, cauliflower, zucchini, peppers, jicama, spinach, cucumbers, cabbage, eggplant, broccoli, spaghetti squash, and collard greens

Seasonings and Condiments: Lemon juice, yellow mustard, salsa, zero-calorie sweeteners, barbecue sauce, cocktail sauce, dried herbs, salt, spices, lime juice, soy sauce, sugar-free syrup, and ½ teaspoons only of ketchup

Summary: The Lean and Green 5&1 plan's homemade meals consist mainly of low-carb veggies, lean proteins, and a few healthy fats. It allows only low-carb beverages like unsweetened almond milk, water, tea, and coffee.

Lean and Green Recipes

Kale Scramble

Servings: 2
Preparation Time: 10 minutes
Cooking Time: 6 minutes
Ingredients:

- 4 eggs
- 1/8 teaspoon ground turmeric
- 1/8 teaspoon red pepper flakes, crushed
- Salt and ground black pepper, as required
- 1 tablespoon water
- 2 teaspoons olive oil
- 1 cup fresh kale, tough ribs removed and chopped

Directions:

1. In a bowl, add the eggs, turmeric, red pepper flakes, salt, black pepper and water and with a whisk, beat until foamy.

2. In a skillet, heat the oil over medium heat

3. Add the egg mixture and stir to combine.

4. Immediately reduce the heat to medium-low and cook for about 1-2 minutes, stirring frequently.

5. Stir in the kale and cook for about 3-4 minutes, stirring frequently.

6. Remove from the heat and serve immediately.

Avocado Toast

Servings: 4
Preparation Time: 15 minutes
Cooking Time: 4 minutes
Ingredients:

- 1 large avocado, peeled, pitted and chopped roughly
- ¼ teaspoon fresh lemon juice
- Salt and ground black pepper, as required
- 4 whole-wheat bread slices
- 4 hard-boiled eggs, peeled and sliced

Directions:

1. In a bowl, add the avocado and with a fork, mash roughly.

2. Add the lemon juice, salt and black pepper and stir to combine well and Set aside.

3. Heat a nonstick frying pan on medium-high heat and toast the slice for about 2 minutes per side.

4. Repeat with the remaining slices.

5. Spread the avocado mixture over each slice evenly.

6. Top each with egg slices and serve immediately.

Tomato & Egg Scramble

Servings: 2
Preparation Time: 10 minutes
Cooking Time: 5 minutes
Ingredients:

- 4 eggs
- ¼ teaspoon red pepper flakes, crushed
- Salt and ground black pepper, as required ¼ cup fresh basil, chopped
- ½ cup tomatoes, chopped
- 1 tablespoon olive oil

Directions:

1. In a large bowl, add eggs, red pepper flakes, salt and black pepper and beat well.

2. Add the basil and tomatoes and stir to combine.

3. In a large non-stick skillet, heat th oil over medium-high heat.

4. Add the egg mixture and cook for about 3-5 minutes, stirring continuously.

5. Serve immediately.

Tofu & Spinach Scramble

Servings: 2
Preparation Time: 10 minutes
Cooking Time: 8 minutes
Ingredients:

- 1 tablespoon olive oil
- 1 garlic clove, minced
- ¼ pound medium-firm tofu, drained, pressed and crumbled 1/3 cup low-sodium vegetable broth
- 2¾ cups fresh baby spinach
- 2 teaspoons low-sodium soy sauce
- 1 teaspoon ground turmeric

- 1 teaspoon fresh lemon juice

Directions:

1. In a frying pan, heat the olive oil over medium-high heat and sauté the garlic for about 1 minute

2. Add the tofu and cook for about 2-3 minutes, slowly adding the broth.

3. Add the spinach, soy sauce and turmeric and stir fry for about 3-4 minutes or until all the liquid is absorbed

4. Stir in the lemon juice and remove from the heat.

5. Serve immediately.

Chicken & Zucchini Pancakes

Servings: 4

Preparation Time: 15 minutes

Cooking Time: 32 minutes

Ingredients:

- 4 cups zucchinis, shredded Salt, as required
- ¼ cup cooked chicken, shredded
- ¼ cup scallion, chopped finely
- 1 egg, beaten
- ¼ cup coconut flour
- Salt and ground black pepper, as required
- 1 tablespoon extra-virgin olive oil

Directions:

1. In a colander, place the zucchini and sprinkle with salt.

2. Set aside for about 8-10 minutes.

3. Squeeze the zucchinis well and transfer into a bowl.

4. In the bowl of zucchini, add the remaining ingredients and mix until well combined.

5. In a large nonstick skillet, heat the oil over medium heat.

6. Add ¼ cup of zucchini mixture into the preheated skillet and spread in an even layer.

7. Cook for about 3-4 minutes per side.

8. Repeat with the remaining mixture.

9. Serve warm.

Baked Eggs

Servings: 6

Preparation Time: 10 minutes

Cooking Time: 9 minutes

Ingredients:

- 2 cups fresh spinach, chopped finely
- 12 large eggs
- ½ cup heavy cream
- ¾ cup low-fat Parmesan cheese, shredded
- Salt and ground black pepper, as required

Directions:

1. Preheat your oven to 425 degrees F.

2. Grease a 12 cups muffin tin.

3. Divide spinach in each muffin cup.

4. Crack an egg over spinach into each cup and drizzle with heavy cream.

5. Sprinkle with salt and black pepper, followed by Parmesan cheese.

6. Bake for approximately 7-9 minutes or until desired doneness of eggs.

7. Serve immediately.

Mini Mac in a Bowl

Servings: 1

Preparation Time: 5 minutes

Cooking Time: 15 minutes

INGREDIENTS:

- 5 oz. lean ground beef
- 2 tablespoons diced white or yellow onion
- 1/8 teaspoon onion powder
- 1/8 teaspoon white vinegar
- 1 oz. dill pickle slices
- 1 teaspoon sesame seed
- 3 cups shredded romaine lettuce
- Cooking spray
- 2 tablespoons reduced-fat shredded cheddar cheese
- 2 tablespoons wish-bone light thousand islands as dressing

Directions:

1. Place a lightly greased small skillet on fire to heat.

2. Add your onion to cook for about 2–3 minutes.

3. Next, add the beef and allow it to cook until it is brown.

4. Next, mix your vinegar and onion powder with the dressing.

5. Finally, top the lettuce with the cooked meat and sprinkle cheese on it. Add your pickle slices.

6. Drizzle the mixture with the sauce and sprinkle the sesame seeds also.

7. Your mini mac in a bowl is ready for consumption.

Zucchini Frittata

Servings: 1
Preparation Time: 20 minutes
Cooking Time: 20 minutes
Ingredients:
- 2 large zucchinis
- ½ teaspoon salt
- 2 eggs
- ½ cup chopped green onions
- 1 cup flour
- ½ teaspoon black pepper
- 1 teaspoon baking powder
- 2 tablespoons oil

Directions:
1. Wash the two zucchinis.
2. Cut off the zucchinis on its ends and grate them in a large mixing bowl.
3. Stir in 1 teaspoon of salt and set aside for about 10 minutes (The salt helps to draw out the water from the zucchinis).
4. Squeeze dry the grated zucchinis to remove as much water as possible.
5. Then followed by the two whole eggs and the chopped green onions.
6. In a bowl, mix a cup of flour, ½ teaspoon of salt, ½ teaspoon of black pepper, and one teaspoon of baking powder.
7. Next, pour the contents of the smaller bowl into those of the larger bowl containing the grated zucchinis.
8. Stir them all together and make sure they are well mixed.
9. Preheat a saucepan to medium temperature and add two tablespoons of oil.
10. Add the zucchini mixture a heaping tablespoonful at a time.
11. Sauté the mixture for about 4 minutes on each side to achieve a golden-brown color.
12. Add more oil to the pan if needed.
13. Serve and enjoy!

Eggs in Bell Pepper Rings

Servings: 2
Preparation Time: 10 minutes
Cooking Time: 6 minutes
Ingredients:
- 1 bell pepper, seeded and cut into 4 (¼-inch) rings
- 4 eggs
- Salt and ground black pepper, as required
- 1 tablespoon fresh parsley, chopped
- 1 tablespoon fresh chives, chopped

Directions:
1. Heat a lightly greased nonstick skillet over medium heat
2. Place 4 bell pepper rings in the skillet and cook for about 2 minutes.
3. Carefully flip the rings.
4. Crack an egg in the middle of each bell pepper ring and sprinkle with salt and black pepper.
5. Cook for about 2-4 minutes or until desired doneness of eggs.
6. Carefully transfer the bell pepper rings ono serving plates and serve with the garnishing of parsley and chives.

Mushroom Omelet

Servings: 5
Preparation Time: 10 Minutes
Cooking Time: 20 Minutes
Ingredients:
- 2 spring onions, chopped
- ½ pound white mushrooms
- Salt and black pepper to the taste
- 4 eggs, whisked
- 1 tablespoon olive oil
- ½ teaspoon cumin, ground
- 1 tablespoon cilantro

Directions:

Heat up a pan with the oil, add the spring onions and the mushrooms, toss and sauté for 5 minutes.

Add the eggs and the rest of the ingredients, toss gently, spread into the pan, cover it, and cook over medium heat for 15 minutes.

Slice the omelet, divide it between plates, and serve for breakfast.

Cauliflower Crust Pizza

Servings: 1

Preparation Time: 15 minutes

Cooking Time: 30 minutes

Ingredients:

- 1/4 cauliflower (it should be cut into smaller portions)
- 1/16 grated parmesan cheese
- 1/2 egg
- ½ teaspoon Italian seasoning
- 1/16 teaspoon kosher salt
- 1cups freshly grated mozzarella
- 1/4 cup spicy pizza sauce
- Basil leaves, for garnishing

Directions:

1. Begin by preheating your oven while using the parchment paper to rim the baking sheet.

2. Process the cauliflower into a fine powder, and then transfer to a bowl before putting it into the microwave.

3. Leave for about 5–6 minutes to get it soft.

4. Transfer the microwaved cauliflower to a clean and dry kitchen towel. Leave it to cool.

5. When cold, use the kitchen towel to wrap the cauliflower and then get rid of all the moisture by wringing the towel. Continue squeezing until the water is gone completely.

6. Put the cauliflower, Italian seasoning, parmesan, egg, salt, and mozzarella (1 cup). Stir very well until well combined.

7. Transfer the combined mixture to the baking sheet previously prepared, pressing it into a 10-inch round shape.

8. Wait for it to bake until it becomes golden in color.

9. Take the baked crust out of the oven and use the spicy pizza sauce and mozzarella (the leftover 1 cup) to top it. Put it again inside the oven for 10 more minutes until the cheese melts and looks bubbly.

10. Garnish using fresh basil leaves. You can also enjoy this with salad.

Apple Omelet

Servings: 1

Preparation Time: 10 minutes

Cooking Time: 9 minutes

Ingredients:

- 2 teaspoons olive oil, divided
- ½ of large green apple, cored and sliced thinly ¼ teaspoon ground cinnamon
- 1/8 teaspoon ground nutmeg
- 2 large eggs
- 1/8 teaspoon vanilla extract
- Pinch of salt

Directions:

1. In a nonstick frying pan, heat 1 teaspoon of oil over medium-low heat

2. Add apple slices and sprinkle with nutmeg and cinnamon.

3. Cook for about 4-5 minutes, turning once halfway through.

4. Meanwhile, in a bowl, add eggs, vanilla extract and salt and beat until fluffy.

5. Add the remaining oil in the pan and let it heat completely.

6. Place the egg mixture over apple slices evenly and cook for about 3-4 minutes or until desired doneness.

7. Carefully turn the pan over a serving plate and immediately fold the omelet

8. Serve hot.

Zucchini Fritters

Servings: 1

Preparation Time: 5 minutes

Cooking Time: 15 minutes

Ingredients:

- 1/4 pound grated zucchini
- 1/4 teaspoon salt
- 1/16 cup grated parmesan
- 1/16 cup flour
- 1/2 cloves minced garlic
- 1/2 tablespoon olive oil
- 1/4 large egg
- Newly ground black pepper and kosher salt to taste

Directions:

1.   Put the grated zucchini into a colander over the sink.

2.   Add your salt and toss it to mix properly, then leave it to settle for about 10 minutes.

3.   Next, use a clean cheesecloth to drain the zucchini completely.

4.   Combine drained zucchini, parmesan, garlic, flour, and the beaten egg in a large bowl, mix, and season with pepper and salt.

5.   Then, pour the olive oil into a skillet applying medium-high heat.

6.   Use a tablespoon to scoop batter for each fritter, put in the oil, and flatten using a spatula.

7.   Allow to cook until the underside is richly golden brown, then flip over to the other side and cook.

8.   Your delicious zucchini fritters are ready to be served.

Veggies Quiche

Servings: 4

Preparation Time: 15 minutes

Cooking Time: 25 minutes

Ingredients:

- 6 large eggs
- Salt and ground black pepper, as required ½ cup unsweetened almond milk
- ½ of onion, chopped
- ¼ cup fresh mushrooms, cut into slices
- ¼ cup red bell pepper, seeded and diced
- 1 tablespoon fresh chives, minced

Directions:

1. Preheat your oven to 350 degrees F.

2. Lightly grease a pie dish.

3. In a bowl, add the eggs, salt, black pepper and coconut oil and beat until well combined.

4. In another bowl, mix together the onion, bell pepper and mushrooms.

5. Transfer the egg mixture into the prepared pie dish evenly.

6. Top with the vegetable mixture evenly.

7. Sprinkle with chives evenly.

8. Bake for approximately 20-25 minutes.

9. Remove the pie dish from oven and set aside for about 5 minutes.

10. Cut into equal-sized wedges and serve.

Broccoli Waffles

Servings: 2

Preparation Time: 10 minutes

Cooking Time: 8 minutes

Ingredients:

- 1/3 cup broccoli, chopped finely
- ¼ cup low-fat Cheddar cheese, shredded
- 1 egg
- ½ teaspoon garlic powder
- ½ teaspoon dried onion, minced
- Salt and ground black pepper, as required

Directions:

1. Preheat a mini waffle iron and then grease it.

2. In a medium bowl, place all ingredients and mix until well combined.

3. Place ½ of the mixture into preheated waffle iron and cook for about 3-4 minutes or until golden brown.

4. Repeat with the remaining mixture.

5. Serve warm.

Green Veggies Quiche

Servings: 4

Preparation Time: 15 minutes

Cooking Time: 20 minutes

Ingredients:

- 6 eggs
- ½ cup unsweetened almond milk
- Salt and ground black pepper, as required
- 2 cups fresh baby spinach, chopped
- ½ cup green bell pepper, seeded and chopped
- 1 scallion, chopped
- ¼ cup fresh cilantro, chopped
- 1 tablespoon fresh chives, minced
- 3 tablespoons low-fat mozzarella cheese, grated

Directions:

1. Preheat your oven to 400 degrees F.

2. Lightly grease a pie dish

3. In a large bowl, add the eggs, almond milk, salt and black pepper and beat until well combined. Set aside.

4. In another bowl, add the vegetables and herbs and mix well.

5. In the bottom of prepared pie dish, place the veggie mixture evenly and top with the egg mixture.

6. Bake for approximately 20 minutes or until a wooden skewer inserted in the center comes out clean.

7. Remove from the oven and immediately sprinkle with the Parmesan cheese.

8. Set aside for about 5 minutes before slicing.

9. Cut into desired sized wedges and serve.

Hearty Veggie Omelet

Servings: 4

Preparation Time: 10 minutes

Cooking Time: 25 minutes

Ingredients:

- 6 large eggs
- ½ cup unsweetened almond milk
- Salt and freshly ground black pepper, to taste
- ½ of onion, chopped
- ¼ cup bell pepper, seeded and chopped
- ¼ cup fresh mushrooms, sliced
- 1 tbsp. chives, minced

Directions:

Preheat the oven to 350°F. Lightly, grease a pie dish.

In a bowl, add eggs, almond milk, salt, and black pepper, and beat until well combined.

In a separate bowl, mix together onion, bell pepper, and mushrooms.

Place the egg mixture into the prepared pie dish evenly and top with vegetable mixture.

Sprinkle with chives evenly.

Bake for about 20–25 minutes.

Remove the pie dish from the oven and set aside for about 5 minutes.

Cut into 4 portions and serve immediately.

Fall Morning Omelet

Servings: 1

Preparation Time: 10 minutes

Cooking Time: 9 minutes

Ingredients:

- 2 tsp. olive oil, divided
- ½ large green apple, cored and sliced thinly

- ¼ tsp. ground cinnamon
- 1/8 tsp. ground nutmeg
- 2 large eggs
- 1/8 tsp. vanilla extract
- Pinch of salt

Directions:

1. In a non-stick frying pan, heat 1 tsp. of oil over medium-low heat.

2. Add apple slices and sprinkle with nutmeg and cinnamon.

3. Cook for about 4–5 minutes, turning once halfway through.

4. Meanwhile, in a bowl, add eggs, vanilla extract, and salt and beat until fluffy.

5. Add the remaining oil to the pan and let it heat completely.

6. Place the egg mixture over apple slices evenly and cook for about 3-4 minutes or until desired doneness.

7. Carefully turn the pan over a serving plate and immediately fold the omelet 8) Serve hot.

Creamy Eggs

Servings: 5

Preparation Time: 10 Minutes

Cooking Time: 15 Minutes

Ingredients:

- 8 eggs, whisked
- 2 spring onions, chopped
- 1 tablespoon olive oil
- ½ cup heavy cream
- Salt and black pepper to the taste
- ½ cup mozzarella, shredded
- 1 tablespoon chives

Directions:

1. Heat up a pan, add the spring onions, toss and sauté them for 3 minutes.

2. Add the eggs mixed with the cream, salt, and pepper and stir into the pan.

3. Sprinkle the mozzarella on top, cook the mix for 12 minutes, divide it between plates, sprinkle the chives on top, and serve.

Lean and Green Chicken Pesto Pasta

Servings: 1

Preparation Time: 5 minutes

Cooking Time: 15 minutes

Ingredients:

- 3 cups raw kale leaves
- 2 tablespoon olive oil
- 2 cups fresh basil
- ¼ teaspoon salt
- 3 tablespoon lemon juice
- 3 garlic cloves
- 2 cups cooked chicken breast
- 1 cup baby spinach
- 6 oz. uncooked chicken pasta
- 3 oz. diced fresh mozzarella
- Basil leaves or red pepper flakes to garnish

Directions:

1. Start by making the pesto, add the kale, lemon juice, basil, garlic cloves, olive oil, and salt to a blender and blend until it is smooth.

2. Add pepper to taste.

3. Cook the pasta and strain off the water. Reserve ¼ cup of the liquid.

4. Get a bowl and mix everything, the cooked pasta, pesto, diced chicken, spinach, mozzarella, and the reserved pasta liquid.

5. Sprinkle the mixture with additional chopped basil or red paper flakes (optional).

6. Now your salad is ready. You may serve it warm or chilled. Also, it can be taken as a salad mix-ins or as a side dish. Leftovers should be stored in the refrigerator inside an airtight container for 3–5 days.

Eggless Scramble

Servings: 2

Preparation Time: 10 minutes

Cooking Time: 8 minutes

Ingredients:

- 1 tbsp. olive oil
- 1 garlic clove, minced
- ¼ lb. medium-firm tofu, drained, pressed, and crumbled
- 1/3 cup vegetable broth
- 2¾ cup fresh baby spinach
- 2 tsp. low-sodium soy sauce
- 1 tsp. ground turmeric
- 1 tsp. fresh lemon juice

Directions:

1. In a frying pan, heat the olive oil over medium-high heat and sauté the garlic for about 1 minute.

2. Add the tofu and cook for about 2–3 minutes, slowly adding the broth.

3. Add the spinach, soy sauce, and turmeric, and stir fry for about 3–4 minutes or until all the liquid is absorbed.

4. Stir in the lemon juice and remove from the heat.

5. Serve immediately.

Tuna Omelet

Servings: 2

Preparation Time: 10 minutes

Cooking Time: 5 minutes

Ingredients:

- 4 eggs
- ¼ cup unsweetened almond milk
- 1 tablespoon scallions, chopped
- 1 garlic clove, minced
- ½ of jalapeño pepper, minced
- Salt and ground black pepper, to taste
- 1 (5-ounce) can water-packed tuna, drained and flaked
- 1 tablespoon olive oil
- 3 tablespoons green bell pepper, seeded and chopped
- 3 tablespoons tomato, chopped
- ¼ cup low-fat cheddar cheese, shredded

Directions:

1. In a bowl, add the eggs, almond milk, scallions, garlic, jalapeño pepper, salt, and black pepper, and beat well.

2. Add the tuna and stir to combine.

3. In a large nonstick frying pan, heat oil over medium heat.

4. Place the egg mixture in an even layer and cook for about 1-2 minutes, without stirring.

5. Carefully lift the edges to run the uncooked portion flow underneath.

6. Spread the veggies over the egg mixture and sprinkle with the cheese.

7. Cover the frying pan and cook for about 30-60 seconds.

8. Remove the lid and fold the omelet in half.

9. Remove from the heat and cut the omelet into 2 portions.

10. Serve immediately.

Bell Pepper Frittata

Servings: 6

Preparation Time: 15 minutes

Cooking Time: 10 minutes

Ingredients:

- 8 eggs
- 1 tablespoon fresh cilantro, chopped
- 1 tablespoon fresh basil, chopped
- ¼ teaspoon red pepper flakes, crushed
- Salt and ground black pepper, as required
- 2 tablespoons olive oil
- 1 bunch scallions, chopped
- 1 cup bell pepper, seeded and sliced thinly ½ cup goat cheese, crumbled

Directions:

1. Preheat the broiler of oven.

2. Arrange a rack in upper third of the oven.

3. In a bowl, add the eggs, fresh herbs, red pepper flakes, salt and black pepper and beat well.

4. In an ovenproof skillet, heat the oil over medium heat and sauté the scallion and bell pepper for about 1 minute.

5. Add the egg mixture over bell pepper mixture evenly and lift the edges to let the egg mixture flowunderneath and cook for about 2-3 minutes.

6. Place the cheese on top in the form of dots.

7. Now, transfer the skillet under broiler and broil for about 2-3 minutes.

8. Remove from the oven and set aside for about 5 minutes before serving.

9. Cut the frittata into desired sized slices and serve.

Cheesy Spinach Waffles

Servings: 4

Preparation Time: 10 minutes

Cooking Time: 20 minutes

Ingredients:

- 1 large egg, beaten
- 1 cup ricotta cheese, crumbled
- ½ cup part-skim Mozzarella cheese, shredded ¼ cup low-fat Parmesan cheese, grated
- 4 ounces frozen spinach, thawed and squeezed dry
- 1 garlic clove, minced
- Salt and ground black pepper, as required

Directions:

1. Preheat a mini waffle iron and then grease it.

2. In a bowl, add all the ingredients and beat until well combined.

3. Place ¼ of the mixture into preheated waffle iron and cook for about 4-5 minutes or until golden brown.

4. Repeat with the remaining mixture.

5. Serve warm.

Chicken & Veggie Frittata

Servings: 8

Preparation Time: 45 minutes

Cooking Time: 15 minutes

Ingredients:

- 1 teaspoon olive oil
- ½ cup yellow onion, sliced
- 2 garlic cloves, minced
- 2 cups fresh spinach, chopped
- 1 cup red bell pepper, seeded and chopped
- 2 cups cooked chicken, chopped
- 2 large eggs
- 4 large egg whites
- 1¼ cups unsweetened almond milk
- 1 cup low-fat cheddar cheese, shredded
- Freshly ground black pepper, as required
- 1 tablespoon Parmesan cheese, shredded

Directions:

1. Preheat your oven to 350 degrees F.

2. Grease a 9-inch pie plate.

3. In a skillet, heat oil over medium heat and sauté onion and garlic for about 2-3 minutes.

4. Add spinach and bell pepper and sauté for about 1-2 minutes.

5. Stir in chicken and transfer the mixture into the prepared pie dish evenly.

6. Add eggs, egg whites, almond milk, cheddar cheese, salt, and black pepper in a mixing bowl and beat until well combined.

7. Pour egg mixture over the chicken mixture evenly and top with Parmesan cheese.

8. Bake for approximately 40 minutes or until top becomes golden brown.

9. Remove the pie dish from oven and set aside for about 5 minutes.

10. Cut into 8 equal-sized wedges and serve.

Zucchini & Carrot Quiche

Servings: 3

Preparation Time: 10 minutes

Cooking Time: 40 minutes

Ingredients:

- 5 eggs
- Salt and ground black pepper, as required
- 1 carrot, peeled and grated
- 1 small zucchini, shredded

Directions:

1. Preheat your oven to 350 degrees F.

2. Lightly grease a small baking dish.

3. In a large bowl, add eggs, salt and black pepper and beat well

4. Add the carrot and zucchini and stir to combine

5. Transfer the mixture into the prepared baking dish evenly

6. Bake for approximately 40 minutes.

7. Remove the baking dish from oven and set aside for about 5 minutes.

8. Cut into equal-sized wedges and serve.

Salmon & Arugula Omelet

Servings: 4

Preparation Time: 10 minutes

Cooking Time: 7 minutes

Ingredients:

- 6 eggs
- 2 tablespoons unsweetened almond milk
- Salt and ground black pepper, as required
- 2 tablespoons olive oil
- 4 ounces smoked salmon, cut into bite-sized chunks
- 2 cups fresh arugula, chopped finely

- 4 scallions, chopped finely

Directions:

1. In a bowl, place the eggs, coconut milk, salt and black pepper and beat well. Set aside.

2. In a nonstick skillet, heat the oil over medium heat.

3. Place the egg mixture evenly and cook for about 30 seconds without stirring.

4. Place the salmon kale and scallions on top of egg mixture evenly.

5. Reduce heat to low and cook, covered for about 4-5 minutes or until omelet is done completely.

6. Uncover the skillet and cook for about 1 minute.

7. Carefully transfer the omelet onto a serving plate and serve.

Romaine Lettuce and Radicchios Mix

Servings: 4

Preparation Time: 6 minutes

Cooking Time: 0 minutes

Ingredients:

- 2 tablespoons olive oil
- A pinch of salt and black pepper
- 2 spring onions, chopped
- 3 tablespoons Dijon mustard
- Juice of 1 lime
- ½ cup basil, chopped
- 4 cups romaine lettuce heads, chopped
- 3 radicchios, sliced

Directions:

1. In a salad bowl, blend the lettuce with the spring onions and the other ingredients, toss and serve.

Fruit Salad

Servings: 4

Preparation Time: 15 minutes

Ingredients:

For Salad

- 4 cups fresh baby arugula
- 1 cup fresh strawberries, hulled and sliced
- 2 oranges, peeled and segmented

For Dressing

- 2 tablespoons fresh lemon juice 2-3 drops liquid stevia
- 2 teaspoons extra-virgin olive oil
- Salt and ground black pepper, as required

Directions:

1. For Salad: in a salad bowl, place all ingredients and mix.

2. For Dressing: place all ingredients in another bowl and beat until well combined.

3. Place dressing on top of salad and toss to coat well.

4. Serve immediately.

Broccoli and Chicken Soup

Servings: 2

Preparation Time: 5 Minutes

Cooking Time: 30 Minutes

Ingredients:

- 4 boneless chicken thighs, diced
- 1 small carrot, chopped
- 1 broccoli head, broken into florets
- 1 garlic clove, chopped
- 1 small onion, chopped
- 4 cups water
- 3 tbsp. extra virgin olive oil
- ½ tsp. salt
- Black pepper, to taste

Directions:

1. In a deep soup pot, heat olive oil and gently sauté broccoli for 2–3 minutes, stirring occasionally.

2. Add in onion, carrot, chicken, and cook, stirring, for 2–3 minutes. Stir in salt, black pepper, and water.

3. Bring to a boil. Simmer for 30 minutes, then remove from heat and set aside to cool.

4. In a blender or food processor, blend soup until completely smooth.

Eggs with Kale & Tomatoes

Servings: 4

Preparation Time: 15 minutes

Cooking Time: 25 minutes

Ingredients:

- 2 tablespoons olive oil
- 1 yellow onion, chopped
- 2 garlic cloves, minced
- 1 cup tomatoes, chopped
- ½ pound fresh kale, tough ribs removed and chopped
- 1 teaspoon ground cumin
- ¼ teaspoon red pepper flakes, crushed
- Salt and ground black pepper, as required
- 4 eggs
- 2 tablespoons fresh parsley, chopped

Directions:

1. In a large nonstick wok, heat the olive oil over medium heat and sauté the onion for about 4-5 minutes.

2. Add in the garlic and sauté for about 1 minute.

3. Add the tomatoes, spices, salt and black pepper and cook for about 2-3 minutes, stirring frequently.

4. Add in the kale and cook for about 4-5 minutes.

5. Carefully crack eggs on top of kale mixture.

6. With the lid, cover the wok and cook for about 10 minutes or until desired doneness of eggs.

7. Serve hot with the garnishing of parsley.

Coleslaw Worth a Second Helping

Servings: 6

Preparation Time: 20 minutes

Cooking Time: 10 minutes

Ingredients:

- 5 cups shredded cabbage
- 2 carrots, shredded
- ½ cup mayonnaise
- ½ cup sour cream
- 3 tablespoons apple cider vinegar
- 1 teaspoon kosher salt
- ½ teaspoon celery seed

Directions:

Add together the cabbage, carrots, and parsley in a large bowl.

Whisk together the mayonnaise, sour cream, vinegar, salt, and celery in a small bowl until smooth. Pour sauce over veggies and pour until covered. Transfer to a serving bowl and bake until ready to serve.

Chicken & Zucchini Muffins

Servings: 4
Preparation Time: 15 minutes
Cooking Time: 15 minutes
Ingredients:

* 4 eggs
* ¼ cup olive oil
* ¼ cup water
* 1/3 cup coconut flour
* ½ teaspoon baking powder ¼ teaspoon salt
* ¾ cup cooked chicken, shredded ¾ cup zucchini, grated
* ½ cup low-fat Parmesan cheese, shredded
* 1 tablespoon fresh oregano, minced
* 1 tablespoon fresh thyme, minced
* ¼ cup low-fat cheddar cheese, grated

Directions:

1. Preheat your oven to 400 degrees F.
2. Lightly grease 8 cups of a muffin pan.
3. In a bowl, add eggs, oil and water and beat until well combined
4. Add the flour, baking powder, and salt, and mix well.
5. Add the remaining ingredients and mix until just combined.
6. Place the muffin mixture into the prepared muffin cup evenly.
7. Bake for approximately 13-15 minutes or until tops become golden brown.
8. Remove muffin pan from oven and place onto a wire rack to cool for about 10 minutes.
9. Invert the muffins onto a platter and serve warm.

Turkey & Veggie Salad

Servings: 4
Preparation Time: 15 minutes
Ingredients:
For Salad:

* 3 cups cooked turkey meat, chopped
* 2 cups, cucumber, chopped
* 1 cup cherry tomatoes, halved
* 1 cup radishes, trimmed and sliced
* 6 cups fresh baby arugula
* 4 tablespoons scallion greens, chopped
* 4 tablespoons fresh parsley leaves, chopped

For Dressing:

* 1 garlic clove, minced
* 3 tablespoons extra-virgin olive oil
* 1 tablespoon balsamic vinegar
* 1 tablespoon fresh lemon juice
* Salt and ground black pepper, as required

Directions:

1. For Salad: in a large serving bowl, add all the ingredients and mix.
2. For Dressing: in another bowl, add all the ingredients and beat till well combined.
3. Pour dressing over salad and gently toss to coat well.
4. Serve immediately.

Mixed Berries Salad

Servings: 4
Preparation Time: 15 minutes
Ingredients:

* 1 cup fresh strawberries, hulled and sliced ½ cups fresh blackberries
* ½ cup fresh blueberries
* ½ cup fresh raspberries
* 6 cup fresh arugula
* 2 tablespoons extra-virgin olive oil
* Salt and ground black pepper, as required

Directions:

1. In a salad bowl, place all the ingredients and toss to coat well.
2. Serve immediately.

Cucumber & Tomato Salad

Servings: 6
Preparation Time: 15 minutes
Ingredients:
For Salad:

* 3 large English cucumbers, sliced thinly sliced
* 2 cups tomatoes, chopped
* 6 cup lettuce, torn

For Dressing:

* 4 tablespoons olive oil
* 2 tablespoons balsamic vinegar
* 1 tablespoon fresh lemon juice
* Salt and ground black pepper, as required

Directions:

1. For Salad: in a large bowl, add the cucumbers, onion and dill and mix.

2. For Dressing: in a small bowl, add all the ingredients and beat until well combined.

3. Place the dressing over the salad and toss to coat well.

4. Serve immediately.

Tofu & Veggie Scramble

Servings: 2

Preparation Time: 15 minutes

Cooking Time: 15 minutes

Ingredients:

* ½ tablespoon olive oil
* 1 small onion, chopped finely
* 1 small red bell pepper, seeded and chopped finely
* 1 cup cherry tomatoes, chopped finely
* 1½ cups firm tofu, crumbled and chopped Pinch of cayenne pepper
* Pinch of ground turmeric Sea salt, to taste

Directions:

1. In a skillet, heat oil over medium heat and sauté the onion and bell pepper for about 4-5 minutes.

2. Add the tomatoes and cook for about 1-2 minutes.

3. Add the tofu, turmeric, cayenne pepper and salt and cook for about 6-8 minutes.

4. Serve hot.

Rocket, Beat & Orange Salad

Servings: 4

Preparation Time: 15 minutes

Ingredients:

* 3 large oranges, peeled, seeded and sectioned
* 2 beets, trimmed, peeled and sliced
* 6 cups fresh rocket
* ¼ cup walnuts, chopped
* 3 tablespoons olive oil
* Pinch of salt

Directions:

1. In a salad bowl, place all ingredients and gently, toss to coat.

2. Serve immediately.

Chicken & Bell Pepper Muffins

Servings: 4

Preparation Time: 15 minutes

Cooking Time: 20 minutes

Ingredients:

* 8 eggs
* Salt and ground black pepper, as required
* 2 tablespoons water
* 8 ounces cooked chicken, chopped finely
* 1 cup green bell pepper, seeded and chopped
* 1 cup onion, chopped

Directions:

1. Preheat your oven to 350 degrees F.

2. Grease 8 cups of a muffin tin.

3. In a bowl, add eggs, black pepper and water and beat until well combined.

4. Add the chicken, bell pepper and onion and stir to combine.

5. Transfer the mixture in prepared muffin cups evenly.

6. Bake for approximately 18-20 minutes or until golden brown.

7. Remove the muffin tin from oven and place onto a wire rack to cool for about 10 minutes.

8. Carefully invert the muffins onto a platter and serve warm.

Blueberries & Spinach Salad

Servings: 4

Preparation Time: 15 minutes

Ingredients:

For Salad:

* 6 cups fresh baby spinach
* 1½ cups fresh blueberries
* ¼ cup onion, sliced
* ¼ cup almond, sliced
* ¼ cup feta cheese, crumbled

For Dressing:

* 1/3 cup olive oil
* 2 tablespoons fresh lemon juice
* ¼ teaspoon liquid stevia
* 1/8 teaspoon garlic powder
* Salt, as required

Directions:

1. For Salad: in a bowl, add the spinach, berries, onion and almonds and mix.

2. For Dressing: in another small bowl, add all the ingredients and beat until well blended.

3. Place the dressing over salad and gently toss to coat well.

4. Serve immediately.

Chicken & Asparagus Frittata

Servings: 4

Preparation Time: 15 minutes

Cooking Time: 12 minutes

Ingredients:

- ½ cup cooked chicken, chopped
- 1/3 cup low-fat Parmesan cheese, grated
- 6 eggs, beaten lightly
- Salt and ground black pepper, as required
- 1 teaspoon coconut oil
- ½ cup boiled asparagus, chopped
- 1 tablespoon fresh parsley, chopped

Directions:

1. Preheat the broiler of oven.

2. In a bowl, add the cheese, eggs, salt and black pepper and beat until well combined.

3. In a large ovenproof skillet, melt coconut oil over medium-high heat and cook the chicken and asparagus for about 2-3 minutes.

4. Add the egg mixture and stir to combine,

5. Cook for about 4-5 minutes.

6. Remove from the heat and sprinkle with the parsley.

7. Now, transfer the skillet under broiler and broil for about 3-4 minutes or until slightly puffed.

8. Cut into desired sized wedges and serve immediately.

Asparagus and Smoked Salmon Salad

Servings: 8

Preparation Time: 15 minutes.

Cooking Time: 10 minutes.

Ingredients:

- 1lb. fresh asparagus, shaped and cut into 1-inch pieces.
- 1/2 cup pecans, smashed into pieces.
- 2heads red leaf lettuce, washed and split.
- 1/2 cup frozen green peas, thawed.
- 1/4 lb. smoked salmon, cut into 1-inch chunks.
- 1/4 cup olive oil.
- 2 tablespoons. lemon juice.
- 1 teaspoon Dijon mustard.
- 1/2 teaspoon salt.
- 1/4 teaspoon pepper.

Directions:

1. Boil a pot of water. Stir in asparagus and cook for 5 minutes until tender. Let it drain; set aside.

2. In a skillet, cook the pecans over medium heat for 5 minutes, constantly stirring until lightly toasted.

3. Combine the asparagus, toasted pecans, salmon, peas, and red leaf lettuce and toss in a large bowl.

4. In another bowl, combine lemon juice, pepper, Dijon mustard, salt, and olive oil. You can coat the salad with the dressing or serve it on its side.

Steak & Tomato Salad

Servings: 5

Preparation Time: 15 minutes

Cooking Time: 15 minutes

Ingredients:

For Steak:

- 2 tablespoons fresh oregano, chopped ½ tablespoon garlic, minced
- 1 tablespoon fresh lemon peel, grated
- ½ teaspoon red pepper flakes, crushed
- Salt and ground black pepper, as required
- 1 (1-pound) (1-inch thick) boneless beef top sirloin steak

For Salad:

- 6 cups fresh salad greens
- 2 cups cherry tomatoes, halved
- 2 tablespoons olive oil
- 2 tablespoons fresh lime juice
- Salt and ground black pepper, as required

Directions:

1. Preheat the gas grill to medium heat.

2. Lightly grease the grill grate.

3. For steak: in a bowl, add the oregano, garlic, lemon peel, red pepper flakes, salt and black pepper and mix well.

4. Rub the steak with garlic mixture evenly.

5. Place the steak onto the grill and cook, covered for about 12-17 minutes, flipping occasionally.

6. Remove the steak from the grill and place onto a cutting board for about 10 minutes.

7. Meanwhile, For Salad: in a large serving bowl, place all ingredients and toss to coat well.

8. Cut the steak into bite-sized pieces.

9. Add the steak pieces into the bowl of salad and toss to coat well.

10. Serve immediately.

Greek Salad

Servings: 5

Preparation Time: 15 Minutes.

Cooking Time: 15 Minutes.

Ingredients:

For Dressing:

- ½ teaspoon black pepper.
- ¼ teaspoon salt.
- ½ teaspoon oregano.
- 1 tablespoon garlic powder.
- 2 tablespoons Balsamic.
- 1/3 cup olive oil.

For Salad:

- ½ cup sliced black olives.
- ½ cup chopped parsley, fresh.
- 1 small red onion, thin-sliced.
- 1 cup cherry tomatoes, sliced.
- 1 bell pepper, yellow, chunked.
- 1 cucumber, peeled, quarter and slice.
- 4 cups chopped romaine lettuce.
- ½ teaspoon salt.
- 2 tablespoons olive oil.
- Directions:

In a small container, join all of the ingredients for the dressing and let this set in the freezer while you make the salad.

To assemble the salad, mix together all the ingredients in a large-sized bowl and toss the veggies gently but thoroughly to mix.

Serve the salad with the dressing in amounts as desired.

Chicken, Kale & Cucumber Salad

Servings: 4

Preparation Time: 15 minutes

Cooking Time: 18 minutes

Ingredients:

For Chicken:

- 1 teaspoon dried thyme
- ½ teaspoon garlic powder
- ½ teaspoon onion powder
- ¼ teaspoon cayenne pepper
- ¼ teaspoon ground turmeric
- Salt and ground black pepper, as required
- 2 (7-ounce) boneless, skinless chicken breasts, pounded into ¾-inch thickness
- 1 tablespoon extra-virgin olive oil

For Salad:

- 5 cups fresh kale, tough ribs removed and chopped
- 1 cup cucumber, chopped
- ½ cup red onion, sliced ¼ cup pine nuts

For Dressing:

- 1 small garlic clove, minced
- 2 tablespoons fresh lemon juice
- 2 tablespoons extra-virgin olive oil
- 1 teaspoon maple syrup
- Salt and ground black pepper, as required

Directions:

1. Preheat your oven to 425 degrees F. Line a baking dish with parchment paper.

2. For chicken: in a bowl, mix together the thyme, spices, salt and black pepper.

3. Drizzle the chicken breasts with oil and then rub with spice mixture generously and drizzle with the oil.

4. Arrange the chicken breasts onto the prepared baking dish.

5. Bake for approximately 16-18 minutes.

6. Remove pan from oven and place the chicken breasts onto a cutting board for about 5 minutes.

7. For Salad: place all ingredients in a salad bowl and mix.

8. For Dressing: place all ingredients in another bowl and beat until well combined.

9. Cut each chicken breast into desired sized slices.

10. Place the salad onto each serving plate and top each with chicken slices.

11. Drizzle with dressing and serve.

Salmon & Veggie Salad

Servings: 2

Preparation Time: 15 minutes

Ingredients:

* 6 ounces cooked wild salmon, chopped
* 1 cup cucumber, sliced
* 1 cup red bell pepper, seeded and sliced ½ cup grape tomatoes, quartered
* 1 tablespoon scallion green, chopped
* 1 cup lettuce, torn
* 1 cup fresh spinach, torn
* 2 tablespoons olive oil
* 2 tablespoons fresh lemon juice

Directions:

1. In a salad bowl, place all ingredients and gently toss to coat well.

2. Serve immediately.

Mixed Veggie Salad

Servings: 6

Preparation Time: 20 minutes

Ingredients:

For Dressing:

* 1 small avocado, peeled, pitted and chopped ¼ cup low-fat plain Greek yogurt
* 1 small yellow onion, chopped
* 1 garlic clove, chopped
* 2 tablespoons fresh parsley
* 2 tablespoons fresh lemon juice

For Salad:

* 6 cups fresh spinach, shredded
* 2 medium zucchinis, cut into thin slices ½ cup celery, sliced
* ½ cup red bell pepper, seeded and sliced thinly ½ cup yellow onion, sliced thinly
* ½ cup cucumber, sliced thinly
* ½ cup cherry tomatoes, halved
* ¼ cup Kalamata olives, pitted
* ½ cup feta cheese, crumbled

Directions:

1. For Dressing: in a food processor, add all the ingredients and pulse until smooth.

2. For Salad: in a salad bowl, add all the ingredients and mix well.

3. Pour the dressing over salad and gently, toss to coat well.

4. Serve immediately.

Eggs with Spinach

Servings: 2

Preparation Time: 10 minutes

Cooking Time: 22 minutes

Ingredients:

* 6 cup fresh baby spinach
* 2-3 tablespoons water
* 4 eggs
* Salt and ground black pepper, as required
* 2-3 tablespoons feta cheese, crumbled

Directions:

1. Preheat your oven to 400 degrees F.

2. Lightly grease 2 small baking dishes.

3. In a large frying pan, add spinach and water over medium heat and cook for about 3-4 minutes.

4. Remove the frying pan from heat and drain the excess water completely.

5. Divide the spinach into prepared baking dishes evenly.

6. Carefully crack 2 eggs in each baking dish over spinach.

7. Sprinkle with salt and black pepper and top with feta cheese evenly.

8. Arrange the baking dishes onto a large cookie sheet.

9. Bake for approximately 15-18 minutes.

10. Serve warm.

Ground Turkey Salad

Servings: 6

Preparation Time: 20minutes

Cooking Time: 13 minutes

Ingredients:

* 1-pound ground turkey
* 1 tablespoon olive oil
* Salt and ground black pepper, as required
* ¼ cup water
* ½ of English cucumber, chopped
* 4 cups green cabbage, shredded

- ½ cup fresh mint leaves, chopped
- 2 tablespoons fresh lime juice
- ¼ cup walnuts, chopped

Directions:

1. Heat oil in a large skillet over medium-high heat and cook the turkey for about 6-8 minutes, breaking up the pieces with a spatula.

2. Stir in the water and cook for about 4-5 minutes or until almost all the liquid is evaporated.

3. Remove from the heat and transfer the turkey into a bowl.

4. Set the bowl aside to cool completely.

5. In a large serving bowl, add the vegetables, mint and lime juice and mix well.

6. Add the cooked turkey and stir to combine.

7. Serve immediately.

Warm Chicken and Avocado Soup

Servings: 2
Preparation Time: 5 Minutes
Cooking Time: 30 Minutes

Ingredients:

- 2 ripe avocados, peeled and chopped
- 1 cooked chicken breast, shredded
- 1 garlic clove, chopped
- 3 cups chicken broth
- Salt and black pepper, to taste
- Fresh coriander leaves, finely cut, to serve
- ½ cup sour cream, to serve

Directions:

Combine avocados, garlic, and chicken broth in a blender.

Process until smooth and transfer to a saucepan. Add in chicken and cook, stirring, over medium heat until the mixture is hot. Serve topped with sour cream and finely cut coriander leaves

Loaded Caesar Salad with Crunchy Chickpeas

Servings: 6
Preparation Time: 5 minutes
Cooking Time: 20 minutes

Ingredients:

For the Chickpeas:

- 2 (15-ounce) cans chickpeas, drained and rinsed
- 2 tablespoons extra-virgin olive oil
- 1 teaspoon kosher salt
- 1 teaspoon garlic powder - 1 teaspoon onion powder
- 1 teaspoon dried oregano

For the Dressing:

- ½ cup mayonnaise - 2 tablespoons grated Parmesan cheese
- 2 tablespoons freshly squeezed lemon juice
- 1 clove garlic, peeled and smashed - 1 teaspoon Dijon mustard
- ½ tablespoon Worcestershire sauce - ½ tablespoon anchovy paste

For the Salad:

- 3 heads romaine lettuce, cut into bite-size pieces

Directions:

To make the chickpeas:

Preheat the oven to 450°F. Line a baking sheet with parchment paper.

Add the chickpeas, oil, salt, garlic powder, onion powder, and oregano in a small container. Scatter the coated chickpeas on the prepared baking sheet.

Roast for about 20 minutes, tossing occasionally, until the chickpeas are golden and have a bit of crunch.

To make the dressing:

In a small bowl, whisk the mayonnaise, Parmesan, lemon juice, garlic, mustard, Worcestershire sauce, and anchovy paste until combined.

To make the salad:

Combine the lettuce and dressing in a large container. Toss to coat. Top with the roasted chickpeas and serve.

Cooking Tip: Don't wash out that bowl you used for the chickpeas—the remaining oil adds a great punch of flavor to blanched green beans or another simply cooked vegetable.

Strawberry & Asparagus Salad

Servings: 8
Preparation Time: 15 minutes
Cooking Time: 5 minutes

Ingredients:

- 2 pounds fresh asparagus, trimmed and sliced
- 3 cups fresh strawberries, hulled and sliced ¼ cup extra-virgin olive oil
- ¼ cup balsamic vinegar
- 2 tablespoons maple syrup
- Salt and ground black pepper, as required

Directions:

1. In a pan of water, add the asparagus over medium-high heat and bring to a boil.

2. Boil the asparagus for about 2-3 minutes or until al dente.

3. Drain the asparagus and immediately transfer into a bowl of ice water to cool completely.

4. Drain the asparagus and pat dry with paper towels.

5. In a large bowl, add the asparagus and strawberries and mix.

6. In a small bowl, add the olive oil, vinegar, honey, salt and black pepper and beat until well blended.

7. Place the dressing over the asparagus strawberry mixture and gently toss to coat.

8. Refrigerate for about 1 hour before serving.

Shrimp Cobb Salad

Servings: 2

Preparation Time: 25 minutes.

Cooking Time: 10 minutes.

Ingredients:

- 4 slices center-cut bacon.
- 1 lb. large shrimp, peeled and deveined.
- 1/2 teaspoon ground paprika.
- 1/4 teaspoon ground black pepper.
- 1/4 teaspoon salt, divided.
- 2 1/2 tablespoons Fresh lemon juice.
- 1 1/2 tablespoons Extra-virgin olive oil.
- 1/2 teaspoon whole-grain Dijon mustard.
- 1 (10 oz.) package romaine lettuce hearts, chopped.
- 2 cups cherry tomatoes, quartered.
- 1 ripe avocado, cut into wedges.
- 1 cup shredded carrots.

Directions:

1. Cook the bacon for 4 minutes on each side in a large skillet over medium heat till crispy.

2. Take away from the skillet and place on paper towels; let cool for 5 minutes. Break the bacon into bits.

3. Throw out most of the bacon fat, leaving behind only 1 tablespoon in the skillet. Bring the skillet back to medium-high heat. Add black pepper and paprika to the shrimp for seasoning. Cook the shrimp around 2 minutes on each side until it is opaque. Sprinkle with 1/8 teaspoon of salt for seasoning.

4. Combine the remaining 1/8 teaspoon of salt, mustard, olive oil, and lemon juice together in a small bowl.

5. Stir in the romaine hearts.

6. On each serving plate, place 1 and 1/2 cups of romaine lettuce. Add on top the same amounts of avocado, carrots, tomatoes, shrimp, and bacon.

Shrimp & Green Beans Salad

Servings: 5

Preparation Time: 20 minutes

Cooking Time: 8 minutes

Ingredients:

For Shrimp:

- 2 tablespoons olive oil
- 2 tablespoons fresh key lime juice
- 4 large garlic cloves, peeled
- 2 sprigs fresh rosemary leaves ½ teaspoon garlic salt
- 20 large shrimp, peeled and deveined

For Salad:

- 1-pound fresh green beans, trimmed ¼ cup olive oil
- 1 onion, sliced
- Salt and ground black pepper, as required
- ½ cup garlic and herb feta cheese, crumbled

Directions:

1. For shrimp marinade: in a blender, add all the ingredients except shrimp and pulse until smooth.

2. Transfer the marinade in a large bowl.

3. Add the shrimp and coat with marinade generously.

4. Cover the bowl and refrigerate to marinate for at least 30 minutes.

5. Preheat the broiler of oven. Arrange the rack in top position of the oven. Line a large baking sheet with a piece of foil.

6. Place the shrimp with marinade onto the prepared baking sheet.

7. Broil for about 3-4 minutes per side.

8. Transfer the shrimp mixture into a bowl and refrigerate until using.

9. Meanwhile, For Salad: in a pan of the salted boiling water, add the green beans and cook for about 3-4 minutes.

10. Drain the green beans well and rinse under cold running water.

11. Transfer the green beans into a large bowl.

12. Add the onion, shrimp, salt and black pepper and stir to combine.

13. Cover and refrigerate to chill for about 1 hour.

14. Stir in cheese just before serving.

Beef & Carrot Stew

Servings: 6

Preparation Time: 15 minutes

Cooking Time: 55 minutes

Ingredients:

- 1½ pounds beef stew meat, trimmed and chopped Salt and ground black pepper, to taste
- 1 tablespoon olive oil
- 1 cup homemade tomato puree
- 4 cups homemade low-sodium beef broth
- 3 carrots, peeled and sliced
- 2 garlic cloves, minced
- ½ tablespoons dried thyme
- 1 teaspoon dried parsley
- 1 teaspoon dried rosemary
- 1 tablespoon paprika
- 1 teaspoon onion powder
- 1 teaspoon garlic powder
- 3 tablespoons fresh parsley, chopped

Directions:

1. In a large bowl, add the beef cubes, salt, and black pepper, and toss to coat well.

2. In a Dutch oven, heat oil over medium-high heat and cook the beef cubes for about 4-5 minutes or until browned.

3. Add in remaining ingredients and stir to combine.

4. Adjust the heat to high and bring to a boil.

5. Now, adjust the heat to low and simmer, covered for about 40-50 minutes.

6. Stir in the salt and black pepper and remove from the heat.

7. Serve hot.

Shrimp & Olives Salad

Servings: 4

Preparation Time: 15 minutes

Cooking Time: 3 minutes

Ingredients:

- 1-pound shrimp, peeled and deveined
- 1 lemon, quartered
- 2 tablespoons olive oil
- 2 teaspoons fresh lemon juice
- Salt and freshly ground black pepper, to taste
- 2 tomatoes, sliced
- ¼ cup onion, sliced
- ¼ cup green olives
- ¼ cup fresh cilantro, chopped finely

Directions:

1. In a pan of lightly salted boiling water, add the quartered lemon.

2. Then, add the shrimp and cook for about 2-3 minutes or until pink and opaque.

3. With a slotted spoon, transfer the shrimp into a bowl of ice water to stop the cooking process.

4. Drain the shrimp completely and then pat dry with paper towels.

5. In a small bowl, add the oil, lemon juice, salt, and black pepper, and beat until well combined.

6. Divide the shrimp, tomato, onion, olives, and cilantro onto serving plates.

7. Drizzle with oil mixture and serve.

Beef & Bok Choy Soup

Servings: 6

Preparation Time: 15 minutes

Cooking Time: 30 minutes

Ingredients:

- 1 tablespoon olive oil
- 1-pound ground beef
- ½ pound fresh mushrooms, sliced
- 1 small yellow onion, chopped
- 1 garlic clove, minced

- 1-pound head bok choy, stalks and leaves separated and chopped
- 2 tablespoons low-sodium soy sauce
- 5 cups low-sodium chicken broth
- Freshly ground black pepper, to taste

Directions:

1. In a large pan, heat oil over medium-high heat and cook the beef for about 5 minutes.

2. Add the onion, mushrooms and garlic and cook for about 5 minutes.

3. Add the bok choy stalks and cook for about 4-5 minutes.

4. Add soy sauce and broth and bring to a boil.

5. Reduce the heat to low. Cover and cook for about 10 minutes.

6. Stir in the bok choy leaves and cook for about 5 minutes.

7. Stir in black pepper and serve hot.

Cucumber & Onion Salad

Servings: 2.

Preparation Time: 10 Minutes.

Cooking Time: 0 Minutes.

Ingredients:

- 3 large cucumbers, sliced thinly.
- ½ cup red onion, sliced.
- 2 tablespoons olive oil.
- 1 tablespoon fresh apple cider vinegar.
- Sea salt, to taste.
- ¼ cup fresh parsley, chopped.

Directions:

1. In a salad bowl, place all the ingredients and toss to coat thoroughly.
2. Serve immediately.

Shrimp, Apple & Carrot Salad

Servings: 4

Preparation Time: 20 minutes

Cooking Time: 3 minutes

Ingredients:

- 12 medium shrimp
- 1½ cups Granny Smith apple, cored and sliced thinly 1½ cups carrot, peeled and cut into matchsticks
- ½ cup fresh mint leaves, chopped
- 2 tablespoons balsamic vinegar

- ¼ cup extra-virgin olive oil
- 1 teaspoon lemongrass, chopped
- 1 teaspoon garlic, minced
- 2 sprigs fresh cilantro, leaves separated and chopped

Directions:

1. In a large pan of the salted boiling water, add the shrimp and lemon and cook for about 3 minutes.

2. Remove from the heat and drain the shrimp well.

3. Set aside to cool.

4. After cooling, peel and devein the shrimps.

5. Transfer the shrimp into a large bowl.

6. Add the remaining all ingredients except cilantro and gently, stir to combine.

7. Cover the bowl and refrigerate for about 1 hour.

8. Top with cilantro just before serving.

Shrimp & Greens Salad

Servings: 6

Preparation Time: 15 minutes

Cooking Time: 6 minutes

Ingredients:

- 3 tablespoons olive oil, divided
- 1 garlic clove, crushed and divided
- 2 tablespoons fresh rosemary, chopped
- 1-pound shrimp, peeled and deveined
- Salt and ground black pepper, as required
- 4 cups fresh arugula
- 2 cups lettuce, torn
- 2 tablespoons fresh lime juice

Directions:

1. In a large wok, heat 1 tablespoon of oil over medium heat and sauté 1 garlic clove for about 1 minute.

2. Add the shrimp with salt and black pepper and cook for about 4-5 minutes.

3. Remove from the heat and set aside to cool.

4. Ina large bowl, add the shrimp, arugula, remaining oil, lime juice, salt and black pepper and gently, toss to coat.

5. Serve immediately.

Fish Stew

Servings: 10
Preparation Time: 15 minutes
Cooking Time: 50 minutes
Ingredients:

- ¼ cup coconut oil
- ½ cup yellow onion, chopped
- 1 cup celery stalk, chopped
- ½ cup green bell pepper, seeded and chopped
- 1 garlic clove, minced
- 4 cups water
- 4 beef bouillon cubes
- 20 ounces okra, trimmed and chopped
- 2 (14-ounce) cans sugar-free diced tomatoes with liquid
- 2 bay leaves
- 1 teaspoon dried thyme, crushed
- 2 teaspoons red pepper flakes, crushed ¼ teaspoon hot pepper sauce
- Salt and ground black pepper, as required
- 32 ounces catfish fillets
- ½ cup fresh cilantro, chopped

Directions:

1. In a large skillet, melt the coconut oil over medium heat and sauté the onion, celery and bell pepper for about 4-5 minutes.

2. Meanwhile, in a large soup pan, mix together bouillon cubes and water and bring to a boil over medium heat.

3. Transfer the onion mixture and remaining ingredients except catfish into the pan of boiling water and bring to a boil.

4. Reduce the heat to low and cook, covered for about 30 minutes.

5. Stir in catfish fillets and cook for about 10-15 minutes.

6. Stir in the cilantro and remove from the heat.

7. Serve hot.

Beef & Cabbage Stew

Servings: 8
Preparation Time: 15 minutes
Cooking Time: 1-hour 5o minutes
Ingredients:

- 2 pounds beef stew meat, trimmed and cubed into 1-inch size
- 1 1/3 cups homemade hot low-sodium chicken broth
- 2 yellow onions, chopped
- 2 bay leaves
- 1 teaspoon Greek seasoning
- Salt and ground black pepper, as required
- 3 celery stalks, chopped
- 1 (8-ounce) package shredded cabbage
- 1 (6-ounce) can sugar-free tomato sauce
- 1 (8-ounce) can sugar-free whole plum tomatoes, chopped roughly with liquid

Directions:

1. Heat a large nonstick pan over medium-high heat and cook the beef for about 4-5 minutes or until browned.

2. Drain excess grease from the pan.

3. Stir in the broth, onion, bay leaves, Greek seasoning, salt and black pepper and bring to a boil.

4. Reduce the heat to low and cook, covered for about 1¼ hours.

5. Stir in the celery and cabbage and cook, covered for about 30 minutes.

6. Stir in the tomato sauce and chopped plum tomatoes and cook, uncovered for about 15-20 minutes.

7. Stir in the salt and remove from heat.

8. Discard bay leaves and serve hot.

Chicken & Kale Soup

Servings: 4
Preparation Time: 15 minutes
Cooking Time: 15 minutes
Ingredients:

- 2 tablespoons extra-virgin olive oil
- ½ of medium onion, chopped
- 3 garlic cloves, minced
- 4 cups homemade low-sodium chicken broth
- 1 cup cooked chicken, cubed
- 1 bunch fresh kale, tough ribs removed and chopped
- 2 tablespoons fresh lemon juice
- Salt and ground black pepper, to taste

Directions:

1. In a soup pan, heat olive oil over medium-high heat and sauté the onion and garlic for about 2-3 minutes.

2. Stir in the cooked chicken and broth and bring to a gentle boil.

3. Now, adjust the heat and to low and simmer for about 3 minutes.

4. Stir in the kale and simmer for 5 minutes or until kale is tender.

5. Stir in the lemon juice, salt and black pepper and remove from the heat.

6. Serve hot.

Asparagus & Parmesan

Servings: 2

Preparation Time: 10 Minutes.

Cooking Time: 6 Minutes.

Ingredients:

- 1 teaspoon sesame oil.
- 11 oz. Asparagus.
- 1 teaspoon chicken stock.
- ½ teaspoon ground white pepper.
- 3 oz. Parmesan.

Directions:

1. Wash the asparagus and chop them roughly.

2. Sprinkle the chopped asparagus with the chicken stock and ground white pepper.

3. Then sprinkle the vegetables with the sesame oil and shake them.

4. Place the asparagus in the air fryer's basket.

5. Cook the vegetables for 4 minutes at 400°F.

6. Meanwhile, shred Parmesan cheese.

7. When the time is over, shake the asparagus gently and sprinkle with the shredded cheese.

8. Cook the asparagus for 2 minutes more at 400°F.

9. After this, transfer the cooked asparagus to the serving plates.

10. Serve and taste it!

Chicken, Kale & Olives Salad

Servings: 4

Preparation Time: 15 minutes

Ingredients:

For Dressing:

- 2 tablespoons fresh orange juice
- 2 tablespoons fresh lemon juice
- 3 tablespoons extra-virgin olive oil
- 1 tablespoon red wine vinegar
- 1 tablespoon honey
- 1 tablespoon fresh orange zest, grated ¾ tablespoon Dijon mustard
- Salt and ground black pepper, as required

For Salad:

- 3 cups cooked chicken, chopped
- 2 cups mixed olives, pitted
- 1 cup red onion, chopped
- 6 cups fresh kale, tough ribs removed and torn

Directions:

1. For Dressing: in a small bowl, add all ingredients and beat well.

2. For Salad: in a large salad bowl, mix together all ingredients.

3. Place dressing over salad and toss to coat well.

4. Serve immediately.

Chicken & Spinach Stew

Servings: 8

Preparation Time: 15 minutes

Cooking Time: 30 minutes

Ingredients:

- 2 tablespoons olive oil
- 1 yellow onion, chopped
- 1 tablespoon garlic, minced
- 1 tablespoon fresh ginger, minced
- 1 teaspoon ground turmeric
- 1 teaspoon ground cumin
- 1 teaspoon ground coriander
- 1 teaspoon paprika
- 1 teaspoon cayenne pepper
- 6 (4-ounce) boneless, skinless chicken thighs, trimmed and cut into 1-inch pieces
- 4 tomatoes, chopped
- 1 (14-ounce) can unsweetened coconut milk Salt and ground black pepper, to taste
- 3 cups fresh spinach, chopped

Directions:

1. In a large heavy-bottomed pan, heat the oil over medium heat and sauté the onion for about 3-4 minutes.

2. Add the ginger, garlic, and spices, and sauté for about 1 minute.

3. Add the chicken and cook for about 4-5 minutes.

4. Add the tomatoes, coconut milk, salt, and black pepper, and bring to gentle simmer.

5. Now, adjust the heat to low and simmer, covered for about 10-15 minutes.

6. Stir in the spinach and cook for about 4-5 minutes.

7. Remove from the heat and serve hot.

Strawberry, Orange & Rocket Salad

Servings: 4

Preparation Time: 15 minutes

Ingredients:

For Salad:

- 6 cups fresh rocket
- 1½ cups fresh strawberries, hulled and sliced
- 2 oranges, peeled and segmented

For Dressing:

- 2 tablespoons fresh lemon juice
- 1 tablespoon raw honey
- 2 teaspoons extra-virgin olive oil
- 1 teaspoon Dijon mustard
- Salt and ground black pepper, as required

Directions:

1. For Salad: in a salad bowl, place all ingredients and mix.

2. For Dressing: place all ingredients in another bowl and beat until well combined.

3. Place dressing on top of salad and toss to coat well.

4. Serve immediately.

Chicken Stuffed Avocado

Servings: 2

Preparation Time: 15 minutes

Ingredients:

- 1 cup cooked chicken, shredded
- 1 avocado, halved and pitted
- 1 tablespoon fresh lime juice

- ¼ cup yellow onion, chopped finely ¼ cup low-fat plain Greek yogurt Pinch of cayenne pepper
- Salt and ground black pepper, as required

Directions:

1. With a small scooper, scoop out the flesh from the middle of each avocado half and transfer into a bowl.

2. In the bowl of avocado flesh, add the lime juice and with a fork, mash until well blended.

3. Add remaining ingredients and stir to combine.

4. Divide the chicken mixture into avocado halves evenly and serve immediately.

Tofu & Veggie Salad

Servings: 8

Preparation Time: 20 minutes

Ingredients:

For Dressing:

- ¼ cup balsamic vinegar
- ¼ cup low-sodium soy sauce
- 2 tablespoons water
- 1 teaspoon sesame oil, toasted
- 1 teaspoon Sriracha
- 3-4 drops liquid stevia

For Salad:

- 1½ pounds baked firm tofu, cubed
- 2 large zucchinis, sliced thinly
- 2 large yellow bell peppers, seeded and sliced thinly
- 3 cups cherry tomatoes, halved
- 2 cups radishes, sliced thinly
- 2 cups purple cabbage, shredded
- 10 cups fresh baby spinach

Directions:

1. For Dressing: in a bowl, add all the ingredients and beat until well combined.

2. Divide the chickpeas, tofu and vegetables into serving bowls.

3. Drizzle with dressing and serve immediately.

Cheddar Potato Gratin

Servings: 2
Preparation Time: 15 Minutes.
Cooking Time: 20 Minutes.
Ingredients:

- 2 potatoes.
- 1/3 cup half and half.
- 1tablespoon oatmeal flour.
- ¼ teaspoon ground black pepper.
- 1 egg.
- 2 oz. Cheddar cheese.

Directions:

1. Wash the potatoes and slice them into thin pieces.
2. Preheat the air fryer to 365°F.
3. Put the potato slices in the air fryer and cook them for 10 minutes.
4. Meanwhile, combine the half and half, oatmeal flour, and ground black pepper.
5. Crack the egg into the liquid and whisk it carefully, then shred the cheddar cheese.
6. When the potato is cooked, take 2 ramekins and place the potatoes on them.
7. Pour the half and half mixture.
8. Sprinkle the gratin with shredded Cheddar cheese.
9. Cook the gratin for 10 minutes at 360°F.
10. Serve the meal immediately.
11. Enjoy!

Turkey Meatballs & Kale Soup

Servings: 6
Preparation Time: 20 minutes
Cooking Time: 25 minutes
Ingredients:
For Meatballs:

- 1-pound lean ground turkey
- 1 garlic clove, minced
- 1 egg, beaten
- ¼ cup low-fat Parmesan cheese, grated
- Salt and ground black pepper, as required

For Soup:

- 1 tablespoon olive oil
- 1 small yellow onion, chopped finely
- 1 garlic clove, minced
- 6 cups low-sodium chicken broth
- 8 cups fresh kale, trimmed and chopped
- 2 eggs, beaten lightly
- Salt and ground black pepper, as required

Directions:

1. For meatballs: in a bowl, add all ingredients and mix until well combined.
2. Make equal-sized small balls from mixture.
3. In a large soup pan, heat oil over medium heat and sauté onion for about 5-6 minutes.
4. Add the garlic and sauté for about 1 minute.
5. Add the broth and bring to a boil.
6. Carefully place the balls in pan and bring to a boil.
7. Reduce the heat to low and cook for about 10 minutes.
8. Stir in the kale and bring the soup to a gentle simmer.
9. Simmer for about 2-3 minutes.
10. Slowly, add the beaten eggs, stirring continuously.
11. Cook for about 1-2 minutes, stirring continuously.
12. Season with the salt and black pepper and remove from the heat.
13. Serve hot.

Cheesy Mushroom Soup

Servings: 4
Preparation Time: 15 minutes
Cooking Time: 15 minutes
Ingredients:

- 2 tablespoons olive oil
- 4 ounces fresh baby Portobello mushroom, sliced
- 4 ounces fresh white button mushrooms, sliced ½ cup yellow onion, chopped
- ½ teaspoon salt
- 1 teaspoon garlic, chopped
- 3 cups low-sodium vegetable broth
- 1 cup low-fat cheddar cheese

Directions:

1. In a medium pan, heat the oil over medium heat and cook the mushrooms and onion with salt for about 5-7 minutes, stirring frequently.
2. Add the garlic, and sauté for about 1-2 minutes.

3. Stir in the broth and remove from the heat.

4. With a stick blender, blend the soup until mushrooms are chopped very finely.

5. In the pan, add the heavy cream and stir to combine.

6. Place the pan over medium heat and cook for about 3-5 minutes.

7. Remove from the heat and serve immediately.

Parmesan Sweet Potato Casserole

Servings: 2

Preparation Time: 15 Minutes.

Cooking Time: 35 Minutes.

Ingredients:

- 2 sweet potatoes, peeled.
- ½ yellow onion, sliced.
- ½ cup cream.
- ¼ cup spinach.
- 2 oz. Parmesan cheese, shredded.
- ½ teaspoon salt.
- 1 tomato.
- 1 teaspoon olive oil.

Directions:

1. Chop the sweet potatoes, the tomato, and the spinach.
2. Spray the air fryer tray with the olive oil.
3. Then place on the layer of the chopped sweet potato.
4. Add the layer of the sliced onion.
5. After this, sprinkle the sliced onion with the chopped spinach and tomatoes.
6. Sprinkle the casserole with the salt and the shredded cheese, then pour the cream.
7. Preheat the air fryer to 390°F.
8. Cover the air fryer tray with the foil.
9. Cook the casserole for 35 minutes.
10. When the casserole is cooked, serve it.
11. Enjoy!

Salty Lemon Artichokes

Servings: 2

Preparation Time: 15 Minutes.

Cooking Time: 45 Minutes.

Ingredients:

- 1 lemon.
- 2 artichokes.
- 1 teaspoon kosher salt.
- 1 garlic head.
- 2 teaspoons olive oil.

Directions:

1. Cut off the edges of the artichokes.
2. Cut the lemon into halves.
3. Peel the garlic head and chop the garlic cloves roughly.
4. Then place the chopped garlic in the artichokes.
5. Sprinkle the artichokes with olive oil and kosher salt.
6. Then squeeze the lemon juice into the artichokes.
7. Wrap the artichokes in the foil.
8. Preheat the air fryer to 330°F.
9. Place the wrapped artichokes in the air fryer and cook for 45 minutes.
10. When the artichokes are cooked, discard the foil and serve.
11. Enjoy!

Chicken & Strawberry Lettuce Wraps

Servings: 2

Preparation Time: 15 minutes

Ingredients:

- 6 ounces cooked chicken breast, cut into strips
- ½ cup fresh strawberries, hulled and sliced thinly
- 1 English cucumber, sliced thinly
- 1 tablespoon fresh mint leaves, minced
- 4 large lettuce leaves

Directions:

1. In a large bowl, add all ingredients except lettuce leaves and gently toss to coat well.

2. Place the lettuce leaves onto serving plates.

3. Place the chicken mixture over each lettuce leaf evenly and serve immediately.

Avocado, Citrus, and Shrimp Salad

Servings: 2

Preparation Time: 15 Minutes.

Ingredients:

* 1 head green leaf lettuce.
* 1 avocado.
* ½pound wild-caught shrimp.
* 2 tablespoons olive oil.
* Juice of 1 lemon.

Directions:

Place the lettuce in a bowl and top with mashed avocado meat.

Clean the shrimps by deveining and removing the head.

Heat oil in a skillet over medium-low heat and heat the oil. Cook the shrimps for 2 minutes on each side.

Place the shrimps on top of mashed avocado and drizzle with lemon juice.

Corn on Cobs

Servings: 2

Preparation Time: 10 Minutes.

Cooking Time: 10 Minutes.

Ingredients:

* 2 fresh corn on cobs.
* 2 teaspoon butter.
* 1 teaspoon salt.
* 1 teaspoon paprika.
* ¼ teaspoon olive oil.

Directions:

1. Preheat the air fryer to 400°F.
2. Rub the corn on cobs with the salt and paprika.
3. Then sprinkle the corn on cobs with olive oil.
4. Place the corn on cobs in the air fryer's basket.
5. Cook the corn on cobs for 10 minutes.
6. When the time is over, transfer the corn on cobs to the serving plates and rub with the butter gently.
7. Serve the meal immediately.
8. Enjoy!

Mozzarella Radish Salad

Servings: 2

Preparation Time: 10 Minutes.

Cooking Time: 20 Minutes.

Ingredients:

* 8 oz. Radish.
* 4 oz. Mozzarella.
* 1 teaspoon balsamic vinegar.
* ½ teaspoon salt.
* 1 tablespoon olive oil.
* 1 teaspoon dried oregano.

Directions:

1. Wash the radish carefully and cut it into halves.
2. Preheat the air fryer to 360°F.
3. Put the radish halves in the air fryer basket.
4. Sprinkle the radish with salt and olive oil.
5. Cook the radish for 20 minutes.
6. Shake the radish after 10 minutes of cooking.
7. When the time is over, transfer the radish to the serving plate.
8. Chop Mozzarella roughly.
9. Sprinkle the radish with Mozzarella, balsamic vinegar, and dried oregano.
10. Stir it gently using two forks.
11. Serve it immediately.

Onion Green Beans

Servings: 2

Preparation Time: 10 Minutes.

Cooking Time: 15 Minutes.

Ingredients:

* 11 oz. green beans.
* 1 tablespoon onion powder.
* 1 tablespoon olive oil.
* ½ teaspoon salt.
* ¼ teaspoon chili flakes.

Directions:

1. Wash the green beans carefully and place them in the bowl.
2. Sprinkle the green beans with the onion powder, salt, chili flakes, and olive oil.
3. Shake the green beans carefully.
4. Preheat the air fryer to 400°F.

5.   Put the green beans in the air fryer and cook for 8 minutes.

6.   After this, shake the green beans and cook them for 4 minutes more at 400°F.

7.   When the time is over, shake the green beans.

8.   Serve the side dish and enjoy!

Spinach & Mushroom Stew

Servings: 4

Preparation Time: 15 minutes

Cooking Time: 30 minutes

Ingredients:

- 2 tablespoons olive oil
- 2 onions, chopped
- 3 garlic cloves, minced
- ½ pound fresh button mushrooms, chopped ¼ pound fresh shiitake mushrooms, chopped ¼ pound fresh spinach, chopped
- Sea salt and freshly ground black pepper, to taste ¼ cup low-sodium vegetable broth
- ½ cup coconut milk
- 2 tablespoons fresh parsley, chopped

Directions:

1. In a large skillet, heat oil over medium heat and sauté the onion and garlic for 4-5 minutes.

2. Add the mushrooms, salt, and black pepper and cook for 4-5 minutes.

3. Add the spinach, broth and coconut milk and bring to a gentle boil.

4. Simmer for 4-5 minutes or until desired doneness.

5. Stir in the cilantro and remove from heat.

6. Serve hot.

Shrimp Stew

Servings: 6

Preparation Time: 15 minutes

Cooking Time: 20 minutes

Ingredients:

- ¼ cup olive oil
- ¼ cup yellow onion, chopped
- ¼ cup green bell pepper, seeded and chopped
- 1 garlic clove, minced
- 1½ pounds raw shrimp, peeled and deveined

- 1 (14-ounce) can diced tomatoes with chilies
- 1 cup unsweetened coconut milk
- 2 tablespoons Sriracha
- 2 tablespoons fresh lime juice
- Salt and ground black pepper, to taste ¼ cup fresh cilantro, chopped

Directions:

1. Heat oil in a pan over medium heat and sauté the onion for about 4-5 minutes.

2. Add the bell pepper and garlic and sauté for about 4-5 minutes.

3. Add the shrimp and tomatoes and cook for about 3-4 minutes.

4. Stir in the coconut milk and Sriracha and cook for about 4-5 minutes.

5. Stir in the lime juice, salt, and black pepper, and remove from the heat.

6. Garnish with cilantro and serve hot.

Fish Stew

Servings: 10

Preparation Time: 15 minutes

Cooking Time: 50 minutes

Ingredients:

- ¼ cup coconut oil
- ½ cup yellow onion, chopped
- 1 cup celery stalk, chopped
- ½ cup green bell pepper, seeded and chopped
- 1 garlic clove, minced
- 4 cups water
- 4 beef bouillon cubes
- 20 ounces okra, trimmed and chopped
- 2 (14-ounce) cans sugar-free diced tomatoes with liquid
- 2 bay leaves
- 1 teaspoon dried thyme, crushed
- 2 teaspoons red pepper flakes, crushed ¼ teaspoon hot pepper sauce
- Salt and ground black pepper, as required
- 32 ounces catfish fillets
- ½ cup fresh cilantro, chopped

Directions:

1. In a large skillet, melt the coconut oil over medium heat and sauté the onion, celery and bell pepper for about 4-5 minutes.

2. Meanwhile, in a large soup pan, mix together bouillon cubes and water and bring to a boil over medium heat.

3. Transfer the onion mixture and remaining ingredients except catfish into the pan of boiling water and bring to a boil.

4. Reduce the heat to low and cook, covered for about 30 minutes.

5. Stir in catfish fillets and cook for about 10-15 minutes.

6. Stir in the cilantro and remove from the heat.

7. Serve hot.

Cheesy Mashed Cauliflower with Bacon

Servings: 6

Preparation Time: 10 Minutes.

Cooking Time: 40 Minutes.

Ingredients:

- 6 slices bacon.
- 2 heads cauliflower, chopped.
- 2 cups water.
- 2 tbsp butter, melted.
- ½ cup buttermilk Salt and black pepper to taste.
- ¼ cup yellow cheddar cheese, grated.
- 2 tbsp chopped chives.

Directions:

1. Preheat oven to 350ºF.

2. Fry bacon in a heated skillet over medium heat for 5 minutes until crispy. Remove to a paper towel-linedplate, allow to cool, and crumble. Set aside and keep bacon fat.

3. Boil the cauliflower in water in a pot over high heat for 7 minutes until tender. Drain and put in a bowl.

4. Include butter, buttermilk, salt, and pepper, and puree using a hand blender until smooth and creamy.

5. Lightly grease a casserole dish with the bacon fat and spread the mash on it. Sprinkle with cheddar cheeseand place under the broiler for 4 minutes on high until the cheese melts. Remove and top with bacon andchopped chives.

6. Serve with pan-seared scallops.

Shrimp Stew

Servings: 6

Preparation Time: 15 minutes

Cooking Time: 20 minutes

Ingredients:

- ¼ cup olive oil
- ¼ cup yellow onion, chopped
- ¼ cup green bell pepper, seeded and chopped
- 1 garlic clove, minced
- 1½ pounds raw shrimp, peeled and deveined
- 1 (14-ounce) can diced tomatoes with chilies
- 1 cup unsweetened coconut milk
- 2 tablespoons Sriracha
- 2 tablespoons fresh lime juice
- Salt and ground black pepper, to taste ¼ cup fresh cilantro, chopped

Directions:

1. Heat oil in a pan over medium heat and sauté the onion for about 4-5 minutes.

2. Add the bell pepper and garlic and sauté for about 4-5 minutes.

3. Add the shrimp and tomatoes and cook for about 3-4 minutes.

4. Stir in the coconut milk and Sriracha and cook for about 4-5 minutes.

5. Stir in the lime juice, salt, and black pepper, and remove from the heat.

6. Garnish with cilantro and serve hot.

Tasty Onion and Cauliflower Dip

Servings: 15

Preparation Time: 20 Minutes.

Cooking Time: 30 Minutes.

Ingredients:

- 1 and ½ cups chicken stock.
- 1 cauliflower head, florets separated.
- ¼ cup mayonnaise.
- ½ cup yellow onion, chopped.
- ¾ cup cream cheese.
- ½ teaspoon chili powder.
- ½ teaspoon cumin, ground.
- ½ teaspoon garlic powder.
- Salt and black pepper to the taste.

Directions:

1.   Put the stock in a pot, add cauliflower and onion, heat up over medium heat, and cook for 30 minutes.

2.   Add chili powder, salt, pepper, cumin, and garlic powder and stir.

3.   Also, add cream cheese and stir a bit until it melts.

4.   Blend using an immersion blender and mix with the mayo.

5.   Transfer to a bowl and keep in the fridge for 2 hours before you serve it.

6.   Enjoy!

Chicken Lettuce Wraps

Servings: 6

Preparation Time: 15 minutes

Cooking Time: 35 minutes

Ingredients:

- pound chicken thighs
- 1 tablespoon olive oil
- ¼ teaspoon garlic powder
- Salt and ground black pepper, as required
- 10 romaine lettuce leaves
- ¾ cup carrot, peeled and julienned ¾ cup cucumber, julienned
- ¼ cup scallion (green part), chopped

Directions:

1. Preheat your oven to 390 degrees F. Line a baking sheet with parchment paper.

2. In a bowl, add the chicken, oil, garlic powder, salt and black pepper and mix well.

3. Arrange the chicken thigh onto the prepared baking sheet in a single layer.

4. Bake for approximately 20-30 minutes or until desired doneness.

5. Remove from the oven and set aside to cool for about 20 minutes.

6. Cut the cooled chicken thighs into bite-sized pieces.

7. In a bowl, add the chicken pieces, celery, parsley, mayonnaise, salt and black pepper and mix until well combined.

8. Arrange the lettuce leaves onto serving plates.

9. Place about ¼ cup of chicken mixture over each lettuce leaf evenly.

10. Top with carrot, cucumber and scallion and serve.

Layered Zucchini & Bell Pepper Bake

Servings: 6

Preparation Time: 10 Minutes.

Cooking Time: 65 Minutes.

Ingredients:

- 2 lb. zucchinis, sliced.
- 2 red bell peppers, seeded and sliced.
- Salt and black pepper to taste.
- 1 ½ cups feta cheese, crumbled.
- 2 tbsp. butter, melted.
- ¼ tsp. xanthan gum.
- ½ cup heavy whipping cream.
- 2 tbsp. fresh dill, chopped.

Directions:

1.   Preheat oven to 370ºF. Place the sliced zucchinis in a colander over the sink, sprinkle with

2.   salt and let sit for 20 minutes.

3.   Transfer to paper towels to drain the excess liquid.

4.   Grease a baking dish with cooking spray and make a layer of zucchini and bell peppers overlapping.

5.   Season with pepper, and sprinkle with feta cheese. Repeat the layering process a second

6.   Combine the butter, xanthan gum, salt, and whipping cream in a bowl. Stir to mix time completely and pour over the vegetables.

7.   Bake for 30–40 minutes or until golden brown on top.

8.   Serve sprinkled with dill.

Orange Chicken

Servings: 6

Preparation Time: 10 minutes

Cooking Time: 20 minutes

Ingredients:

- 3 garlic cloves, minced
- ½ cup fresh orange juice
- 1 tablespoon apple cider vinegar
- 2 tablespoons low-sodium soy sauce ¼ teaspoon ground ginger
- ¼ teaspoon ground cinnamon
- Freshly ground black pepper, to taste

- 2 pounds skinless, bone-in chicken thighs
  1/3 cup scallion, sliced

Directions:

1. For marinate in a large bowl, mix together all ingredients except for chicken thighs and scallion.

2. Add the chicken thighs and coat with marinade generously.

3. Cover the bowl and refrigerate to marinate for about 4 hours.

4. Remove the chicken from bowl, reserving marinade.

5. Heat a lightly greased large non-stick skillet over medium-high heat and cook the chicken thighs for about 5-6 minutes or till golden brown.

6. Flip the side and cook for about 4 minutes.

7. Stir in the reserved marinade and bring to a boil.

8. Reduce the heat to medium-low and cook, covered for about 6-8 minutes or until sauce becomes thick.

9. Stir in the scallion and remove from the heat.

10. Serve hot

Carrot Lentil Burgers

Servings: 2

Preparation Time: 10 Minutes.
Cooking Time: 15 Minutes.

Ingredients:

- 6 oz. lentils, cooked.
- 1 egg.
- 2 oz. carrot, grated.
- 1 teaspoon semolina.
- ½ teaspoon salt.
- 1 teaspoon turmeric.
- 1 tablespoon butter.

Directions:

1. Crack the egg into the bowl and whisk it.

2. Add the cooked lentils and mash the mixture with the help of the fork.

3. Then sprinkle the mixture with the grated carrot, semolina, salt, and turmeric.

4. Mix it up and make the medium burgers.

5. Put the butter into the lentil burgers. It will make them juicy.

6. Preheat the air fryer to 360°F.

7. Put the lentil burgers in the air fryer and cook for 12 minutes.

8. Flip the burgers into another side after 6 minutes of cooking.

9. Then chill the cooked lentil burgers and serve them.

10. Enjoy!

Chicken Burgers

Servings: 4

Preparation Time: 15 minutes
Cooking Time: 10 minutes

Ingredients:

For Burgers:

- 1¼ pounds ground chicken
- 1 egg
- ½ yellow onion, grated
- Salt and ground black pepper, as required
- 1 teaspoon dried thyme
- 2 tablespoons olive oil

For Serving:

- 4 cups lettuce, torn
- 1 cucumber, chopped

Directions:

1. In a bowl, add all the ingredients and mix until well combined.

2. Make 8 small equal-sized patties from the mixture.

3. In a large frying pan, heat the oil over medium heat and cook the patties for about 4-5 minutes per side or until done completely.

4. Divide the lettuce and cucumber onto serving plates and top each with 2 burgers.

5. Serve hot.

Lemony Chicken Thighs

Servings: 4

Preparation Time: 10 minutes
Cooking Time: 16 minutes

Ingredients:

- 2 tablespoons olive oil, divided
- 1 tablespoon fresh lemon juice
- 1 tablespoon lemon zest, grated
- 2 teaspoons dried oregano
- 1 teaspoon dried thyme
- Salt and ground black pepper, to taste

- 1½ pounds bone-in chicken thighs
- 6 cups fresh baby spinach

Directions:

1. Preheat your oven to 420 degree F.

2. Add 1 tablespoon of the oil, lemon juice, lemon zest, dried herbs, salt, and black pepper in a large mixing bowl and mix well.

3. Add the chicken thighs and coat with the mixture generously.

4. Refrigerate to marinate for at least 20 minutes.

5. In an oven-proof wok, heat the remaining oil over medium-high heat and sear the chicken thighs for about 2-3 minutes per side.

6. Immediately transfer the wok into the oven and Bake for approximately 10 minutes.

7. Serve hot alongside the spinach.

Stuffed Chicken Breast

Servings: 4

Preparation Time: 15 minutes

Cooking Time: 25 minutes

Ingredients:

- 1 tablespoon olive oil
- 1 small onion, chopped
- 1 pepperoni pepper, seeded and sliced thinly
- ½ of red bell pepper, seeded and sliced thinly
- 2 teaspoons garlic, minced
- 1 cup fresh spinach, trimmed and chopped ½ teaspoon dried oregano
- Salt and ground black pepper, as required
- 4 (5-ounce) skinless, boneless chicken breasts, butterflied and pounded

Directions:

1. Preheat your oven to 350 degrees F.

2. Line a baking sheet with parchment paper.

3. In a saucepan, heat the olive oil over medium heat and sauté onion and both peppers for about 1 minute.

4. Add the garlic and spinach and cook for about 2-3 minutes or until just wilted.

5. Stir in oregano, salt and black pepper and remove the saucepan from heat.

6. Place the chicken mixture into the middle of each butterflied chicken breast.

7. Fold each chicken breast over filling to make a little pocket and secure with toothpicks.

8. Arrange the chicken breasts onto the prepared baking sheet.

9. Bake for approximately 18-20 minutes.

10. Serve warm.

Chicken with Broccoli

Servings: 4

Preparation Time: 15 minutes

Cooking Time: 22 minutes

Ingredients:

- 2 tablespoons olive oil, divided
- 4 (4-ounce) boneless, skinless chicken breasts, cut into small pieces Salt and freshly ground black pepper, to taste
- 1 onion, chopped finely
- 1 teaspoon fresh ginger, grated
- 1 teaspoon garlic, minced
- 1 cup broccoli florets
- 1½ cups fresh mushrooms, sliced
- 8 ounces low-sodium chicken broth

Directions:

1. In a large skillet, heat 1 tablespoon of oil over medium-high heat and stir fry the chicken pieces, salt, and black pepper for about 4-5 minutes or until golden brown.

2. With a slotted spoon, transfer the chicken onto a plate.

3. In the same skillet, heat the remaining oil over medium-high heat and sauté the onion, ginger, and garlic for about 4-5 minutes.

4. Add in mushrooms and cook for about 4-5 minutes, stirring frequently.

5. Add the broccoli and stir fry for about 3 minutes.

6. Add the cooked chicken and broth and stir fry for about 3-5 minutes

7. Add in the salt and black pepper and remove from the heat.

8. Serve hot.

Spicy Beef Koftas

Servings: 6

Preparation Time: 15 minutes

Cooking Time: 10 minutes

Ingredients:

- 1-pound ground beef
- 2 tablespoons low-fat plain Greek yogurt

- 2 tablespoons yellow onion, grated
- 2 teaspoons garlic, minced
- 2 tablespoons fresh cilantro, minced
- 1 teaspoon ground coriander
- 1 teaspoon ground cumin
- 1 teaspoon ground turmeric
- Salt and ground black pepper, as required
- 1 tablespoon olive oil
- 8 cups fresh salad greens

Directions:

1. In a large bowl, add all the ingredients except for greens and mix until well combined.

2. Make 12 equal-sized oblong patties from the mixture.

3. In a large non-stick skillet, heat the oil over medium-high heat and cook the patties for about 10 minutes or until browned from both sides, flipping occasionally.

4. Meanwhile, for sauce: in a bowl, add all the ingredients and mix until well combined.

5. Serve the Koftas with the yogurt sauce.

Balsamic Chicken Breast

Servings: 4
Preparation Time: 10 minutes
Cooking Time: 14 minutes

Ingredients:

- ¼ cup balsamic vinegar
- 2 tablespoons olive oil
- 1½ teaspoons fresh lemon juice
- ½ teaspoon lemon-pepper seasoning
- 4 (6-ounce) boneless, skinless chicken breast halves, pounded slightly
- 6 cups fresh baby kale

Directions:

1. In a glass baking dish, place the vinegar, oil, lemon juice and seasoning and mix well.

2. Add the chicken breasts and coat with the mixture generously.

3. Refrigerate to marinate for about 25-30 minutes.

4. Preheat the grill to medium heat.

5. Grease the grill grate.

6. Remove the chicken from bowl and discard the remaining marinade.

7. Place the chicken breasts onto the grill and cover with the lid.

8. Cook for about 5-7 minutes per side or until desired doneness.

9. Serve hot alongside the kale.

Eggplant Ratatouille

Servings: 2
Preparation Time: 15 Minutes.
Cooking Time: 15 Minutes.

Ingredients:

- 1 eggplant.
- 1 sweet yellow pepper.
- 3 cherry tomatoes.
- 1/3 white onion, chopped.
- ½ teaspoon garlic clove, sliced.
- 1 teaspoon olive oil.
- ½ teaspoon ground black pepper.
- ½ teaspoon Italian seasoning.

Directions:

1. Preheat the air fryer to 360°F.

2. Peel the eggplants and chop them.

3. Put the chopped eggplants in the air fryer basket.

4. Chop the cherry tomatoes and add them to the air fryer basket.

5. Then add chopped onion, sliced garlic clove, olive oil, ground black pepper, and Italian seasoning.

6. Chop the sweet yellow pepper roughly and add it to the air fryer basket.

7. Shake the vegetables gently and cook for 15 minutes.

8. Stir the meal after 8 minutes of cooking.

9. Transfer the cooked ratatouille to the serving plates.

10. Enjoy!

Spiced Beef Meatballs

Servings: 4
Preparation Time: 15 minutes
Cooking Time: 20 minutes

Ingredients:

- 1-pound ground beef
- 1 tablespoon olive oil
- 1 teaspoon dehydrated onion flakes, crushed
  ½ teaspoon granulated garlic
- ½ teaspoon ground cumin

- ½ teaspoon red pepper flakes, crushed Salt, as required
- 6 cups fresh baby spinach
- 1 cup tomato, chopped

Directions:

1. Preheat the oven to 400 degrees F.

2. Line a larger baking sheet with parchment paper.

3. In a mixing bowl, place all the ingredients and with your hands, mix until well combined.

4. Shape the mixture into desired and equal-sized balls.

5. Arrange meatballs into the prepared baking sheet in a single layer and Bake for approximately 15-20minutes or until done completely.

6. Serve hot alongside spinach and tomato.

Moist Shredded Beef

Servings: 8

Preparation Time: 10 minutes.

Cooking Time: 20 minutes.

Ingredients:

- 2 lbs. beef chuck roast, cut into chunks.
- 1/2 tbsp. dried red pepper.
- 1 tbsp. Italian seasoning.
- 1 tbsp garlic, minced.
- 2 tbsp. vinegar.
- 14 oz. can fire-roasted tomatoes.
- 1/2 cup bell pepper, chopped.
- 1/2 cup carrots, chopped.
- 1 cup onion, chopped.
- 1 tsp. salt.

Directions:

1. Add all ingredients into the inner pot of the instant pot and set the pot on sauté mode.

2. Seal pot with lid and cook on high for 20 minutes.

3. Once done, release pressure using quick release. Remove lid.

4. Shred the meat using a fork.

5. Stir well and serve.

Hearty Beef Ragu

Servings: 4

Preparation Time: 10 minutes.

Cooking Time: 50 minutes.

Ingredients:

- 1 1/2 lbs. beef steak, diced.
- 1 1/2 cup beef stock.
- 1 tbsp. coconut amino.
- 4 oz. can tomatoes, chopped.
- 1/2 tsp. ground cinnamon.
- 1 tsp dried thyme.
- 1 tsp. dried basil.
- 1 tsp. paprika.
- 1 bay leaf.
- 1 tbsp. garlic, chopped.
- 1/2 tsp. cayenne pepper.
- 1 celery stick, diced.
- 1 carrot, diced.
- 1 onion, diced.
- 2 tbsp. olive oil.
- 1/4 tsp. pepper.
- 1/2 tsp. sea salt.

Directions:

1. Add oil into the instant pot and set the pot on sauté mode.

2. Add celery, carrots, onion, and salt and sauté for 5 minutes.

3. Add meat and remaining ingredients and stir everything well.

4. Seal pot with lid and cook on high for 30 minutes.

5. Once done, allow to release pressure naturally for 10 minutes, then release remaining using quick release.

6. Remove lid.

7. Shred meat using a fork. Set pot on sauté mode and cook for 10 minutes. Stir every 2–3 minutes.

8. Serve and enjoy.

Beef & Spinach Burgers

Servings: 4

Preparation Time: 15 minutes

Cooking Time: 12 minutes

Ingredients:

For Burgers:

- 1-pound ground beef
- 1 cup fresh baby spinach leaves, chopped
- ½ of small yellow onion, chopped

- ¼ cup sun-dried tomatoes, chopped
- 1 egg, beaten
- ¼ cup feta cheese, crumbled
- Salt and ground black pepper, as required
- 2 tablespoons olive oil

For Serving:

- 3 cups fresh spinach, torn
- 3 cups lettuce, torn
- 2 tomatoes, sliced

Directions:

1. For Burgers: in a large bowl, add all ingredients except for oil and mix until well combined.

2. Make 4 equal-sized patties from the mixture.

3. In a skillet, heat the oil over medium-high heat and cook the patties for about 5-6 minutes per side or until desired doneness.

4. Divide the lettuce, spinach, and tomato slices and onto serving plates.

5. Top each with 1 burger and serve.

Chicken & Veggies Casserole

Servings: 4

Preparation Time: 15 minutes
Cooking Time: 25 minutes

Ingredients:

- 1 tablespoon olive oil
- 1 small onion, chopped
- 1 pepperoni pepper, seeded and sliced thinly
- ½ of red bell pepper, seeded and sliced thinly
- 2 teaspoons garlic, minced
- 1 cup fresh spinach, trimmed and chopped
  ½ teaspoon dried oregano
- Salt and freshly ground black pepper, to taste
- 4 (5-ounce) skinless, boneless chicken breasts, butterflied and pounded

Directions:

1. Preheat your oven to 350 degrees F.

2. Line a baking sheet with parchment paper.

3. In a saucepan, heat the olive oil over medium heat and sauté onion and both peppers for about 1 minute.

4. Add the garlic and spinach and cook for about 2-3 minutes or until just wilted.

5. Stir in oregano, salt and black pepper and remove the saucepan from heat.

6. Place the chicken mixture into the middle of each butterflied chicken breast.

7. Fold each chicken breast over filling to make a little pocket and secure with toothpicks.

8. Arrange the chicken breasts onto the prepared baking sheet.

9. Bake for approximately 18-20 minutes.

10. Serve hot.

Chicken & Green Veggies Curry

Servings: 4

Preparation Time: 15 minutes
Cooking Time: 30 minutes

Ingredients:

- 1-pound skinless, boneless chicken breasts, cubed
- 1 tablespoon olive oil
- 2 tablespoons green curry paste
- 1 cup unsweetened coconut milk
- 1 cup low-sodium chicken broth
- 1 cup asparagus spears, trimmed
- 1 cup green beans, trimmed
- Salt and ground black pepper, as required
- ¼ cup fresh cilantro leaves, chopped

Directions:

1. In a skillet, heat oil over medium heat and sauté the curry paste for about 1-2 minutes.

2. Add the chicken and cook for about 8-10 minutes.

3. Add coconut milk and broth and bring to a boil.

4. Reduce the heat low and cook for about 8-10 minutes.

5. Add asparagus, green beans, salt and black pepper and cook for about 4-5 minutes or until desired doneness.

6. Serve hot.

Turkey with Peas

Servings: 6

Preparation Time: 15 minutes
Cooking Time: 40 minutes

Ingredients:

- 2 tablespoons extra virgin olive oil 1-pound lean ground turkey

- 1 large white onion, chopped finely
- 2 garlic cloves, minced
- ½ tablespoon fresh ginger, minced
- 1 teaspoon ground coriander
- 1 teaspoon ground cumin
- ¼ teaspoon chili powder
- 2 medium tomatoes, seeded and chopped
- ½ cup low-sodium chicken broth
- Salt and freshly ground black pepper, to taste
- 2 cups fresh peas, shelled
- 2 tablespoons fresh cilantro, chopped

Directions:

1. In a large skillet, heat the oil over medium heat and cook the turkey for about 4-5 minutes or until browned completely.

2. With a slotted spoon, transfer the turkey into a large bowl.

3. In the same skillet, add the onion and sauté for about 4-6 minutes.

4. Add the garlic, ginger, coriander, cumin and chili powder and sauté for about 1 minute.

5. Add the tomatoes and cook for about 2-3 minutes, crushing completely with the back of spoon.

6. Stir in the cooked turkey, broth, salt and black pepper and bring to a boil.

7. Reduce the heat to medium-low and simmer, covered for about 8-10 minutes, stirring occasionally.

8. Stir in peas and cook for about 15-20 minutes.

9. Remove from the heat and serve hot with the garnishing of almonds and cilantro leaves.

Beef & Broccoli Bowl

Servings: 1

Preparation Time: 15 minutes

Cooking Time: 12 minutes

Ingredients:

- 4 ounces lean ground beef
- 1 cup broccoli, cut into bite-sized pieces
- 2 tablespoons low-sodium chicken broth ¼ cup tomatoes, chopped
- ¼ teaspoon onion powder
- ¼ teaspoon garlic powder
- Pinch of red pepper flakes

- Salt, to taste
- 1 ounce low-fat cheddar cheese

Directions:

1. Heat a lightly greased skillet over medium heat and cook the beef for about 8-10 minutes or until browned completely.

2. Meanwhile, in a microwave-safe bowl, place the broccoli and broth.

3. With a plastic wrap, cover the bowl and microwave for about 4 minutes.

4. Remove from the microwave and set aside.

5. Drain the grease from skillet.

6. Add the tomatoes, garlic powder, onion powder, red pepper flakes and salt and stir to combine well.

7. Add the broccoli and toss to coat well.

8. Remove from the heat and transfer the beef mixture into a serving bowl.

9. Top with cheddar cheese and serve.

Spicy Beef Burgers

Servings: 4

Preparation Time: 20 minutes

Cooking Time: 10 minutes

Ingredients:

For Burgers

- 1-pound lean ground beef
- ¼ cup fresh parsley, chopped
- ¼ cup fresh parsley, chopped
- ¼ cup fresh cilantro, chopped
- 1 tablespoon fresh ginger, chopped
- 1 teaspoon ground cumin
- 1 teaspoon ground coriander
- ½ teaspoon ground cinnamon
- Salt and ground black pepper, as required

For Salad:

- 6 cup fresh baby arugula
- 2 cups cherry tomatoes, quartered
- 1 tablespoon fresh lemon juice
- 1 tablespoon extra-virgin olive oil

Directions:

1. In a bowl, add the beef, ¼ cup of parsley, cilantro, ginger, spices, salt and black pepper and mix until well combined.

2. Make 4 equal-sized patties from the mixture.

3. Heat a greased grill pan over medium-high heat and cook the patties for about 3 minutes per side or until desired doneness.

4. Meanwhile, in a bowl, add arugula, tomatoes, lemon juice and oil and toss to coat well.

5. Divide the salad onto serving plates and top each with 1 patty.

6. Serve immediately.

Chicken & Cauliflower Curry

Servings: 6

Preparation Time: 15 minutes

Cooking Time: 20 minutes

Ingredients:

- ¼ cup olive oil
- 3 garlic cloves, minced
- 2 tablespoons curry powder
- 1½ pounds skinless, boneless chicken thighs, cut into bite-sized pieces Salt and ground black pepper, as required
- 1-pound cauliflower, cut into small pieces
- 1 green bell pepper, seeded and chopped
- 14 ounces unsweetened coconut milk ¼ cup fresh parsley, chopped

Directions:

1. In a large skillet, heat the oil over medium heat and sauté the garlic and curry powder for about 1 minute.

2. Add the chicken, salt and black pepper and cook for about 5-6 minutes, stirring frequently.

3. With a slotted spoon, transfer the chicken onto a plate.

4. In the skillet, add the cauliflower and bell pepper and cook for about 2-3 minutes.

5. Add the coconut milk and simmer for about 5-7 minutes.

6. Stir in the cooked chicken, salt and black pepper and cook for about 2-3 minutes.

7. Serve hot with the garnishing of parsley.

Garlicky Beef Tenderloin

Servings: 19

Preparation Time: 10 minutes

Cooking Time: 50 minutes

Ingredients:

- 1 (3-pound) center-cut beef tenderloin roast
- 4 garlic cloves, minced
- 1 tablespoon fresh rosemary, minced
- Salt and ground black pepper, to taste
- 1 tablespoon olive oil
- 15 cups fresh spinach

Directions:

1. Preheat your oven to 425 degree F.

2. Grease a large shallow roasting pan.

3. Place the roast into the prepared roasting pan.

4. Rub the roast with garlic, rosemary, salt, and black pepper, and drizzle with oil.

5. Roast the beef for about 45-50 minutes.

6. Remove from oven and place the roast onto a cutting board for about 10 minutes.

7. With a knife, cut beef tenderloin into desired-sized slices and serve alongside the spinach.

Simple Steak

Servings: 4

Preparation Time: 10 minutes

Cooking Time: 10 minutes

Ingredients:

- 1 tablespoon olive oil
- 4 (6-ounce) flank steaks
- Salt and ground black pepper, to taste
- 6 cups fresh salad greens

Directions:

1. In a wok, heat the oil over medium-high heat and cook steaks with salt and black pepper for about 3-5 minutes per side.

2. Transfer the steaks onto serving plates and serve alongside the greens.

Tasty Beef Stew

Servings: 4

Preparation Time: 10 minutes.

Cooking Time: 30 minutes.

Ingredients:

- 2 1/2 lbs. beef roast, cut into chunks.
- 1 cup beef broth.
- 1/2 cup balsamic vinegar.
- 1 tbsp. honey.
- 1/2 tsp. red pepper flakes.
- 1tbsp. garlic, minced.
- Pepper.
- Salt.

Directions:

1.   Add all ingredients into the inner pot of the instant pot and stir well.

2.   Seal pot with lid and cook on high for 30 minutes.

3.   Once done, allow to release pressure naturally. Remove lid.

4.   Stir well and serve.

Meatloaf

Servings: 6

Preparation Time: 10 minutes.

Cooking Time: 35 minutes.

Ingredients:

*   2 lbs. ground beef.
*   2 eggs, lightly beaten.
*   1/4 tsp. dried basil.
*   3 tbsp. olive oil.
*   1/2 tsp. dried sage.
*   1 1/2 tsp. dried parsley.
*   1tsp. oregano.
*   2 tsp. thyme.
*   1 tsp. rosemary.
*   Pepper.
*   Salt.

Directions:

1.   Pour 1 1/2 cups of water into the instant pot, then place the trivet in the pot.

2.   Spray loaf pan with cooking spray.

3.   Add all ingredients into the mixing bowl and mix until well combined.

4.   Transfer meat mixture into the prepared loaf pan and place loaf pan on top of the trivet in the pot.

5.   Seal pot with lid and cook on high for 35 minutes.

6.   Once done, allow to release pressure naturally for 10 minutes, then release remaining using quick release.

7.   Remove lid.

8.   Serve and enjoy.

Spicy Beef Chili Verde

Servings: 2

Preparation Time: 10 minutes.

Cooking Time: 23 minutes.

Ingredients:

*   1/2 lb. beef stew meat, cut into cubes.
*   1/4 tsp. chili powder.
*   1 tbsp. olive oil.
*   1 cup chicken broth.
*   1 Serrano pepper, chopped.
*   1 tsp. garlic, minced.
*   1 small onion, chopped.
*   1/4 cup grape tomatoes, chopped.
*   1/4 cup tomatillos, chopped.
*   Pepper.
*   Salt.

Directions:

1.   Add oil into the instant pot and set the pot on sauté mode.

2.   Add garlic and onion and sauté for 3 minutes.

3.   Add remaining ingredients and stir well.

4.   Seal pot with lid and cook on high for 20 minutes.

5.   Once done, allow to release pressure naturally. Remove lid.

6.   Stir well and serve.

Carrot Mushroom Beef Roast

Servings: 4

Preparation Time: 10 minutes.

Cooking Time: 40 minutes.

Ingredients:

*   1 1/2 lbs. beef roast.
*   1 tsp. paprika.
*   1/4 tsp. dried rosemary.
*   1 tsp. garlic, minced.
*   1/2 lb. mushrooms, sliced.
*   1/2 cup chicken stock.
*   2 carrots, sliced.
*   Pepper.
*   Salt.

Directions:

1.   Add all ingredients into the inner pot of the instant pot and stir well.

2.   Seal pot with lid and cook on high for 40 minutes.

3.   Once done, allow to release pressure naturally for 10 minutes, then release remaining using quick release.

4. Remove lid.

5. Slice and serve.

Spiced Flank Steak

Servings: 5

Preparation Time: 10 minutes

Cooking Time: 20 minutes

Ingredients:

- ½ teaspoons dried thyme, crushed
- ½ teaspoons dried oregano, crushed
- 1 teaspoon red chili powder
- ½ teaspoons ground cumin
- ¼ teaspoons garlic powder
- Salt and ground black pepper, to taste
- 1½ pounds flank steak, trimmed
- 6 cups salad greens

Directions:

1. In a large bowl, add the dried herbs and spices and mix well.

2. Add the steaks and rub with mixture generously.

3. Set aside for about 15-20 minutes.

4. Preheat the grill to medium heat. Grease the grill grate.

5. Place the steak onto the grill over medium coals and cook for about 18-20 minutes, flipping once halfway through.

6. Remove the steak from grill and place onto a cutting board for about 10 minutes before slicing.

7. With a knife, cut steak into desired sized slices and serve alongside the greens.

Steak with Green Beans

Servings: 2

Preparation Time: 15 minutes

Cooking Time: 10 minutes

Ingredients:

For Steak:

- 2 (5-ounce) sirloin steaks, trimmed
- Salt and ground black pepper, as required
- 1 tablespoon extra-virgin olive oil
- 1 garlic clove, minced

For Green Beans:

- ½ pound fresh green beans
- ½ tablespoon olive oil

- ½ tablespoon fresh lemon juice

Directions:

1. For steak: season the steaks with salt and black pepper evenly.

2. In a cast iron sauté pan, heat the olive oil over high heat and sauté garlic for about 15-20 seconds.

3. Add the steaks and cook for about 3 minutes per side.

4. Flip the steaks and cook for about 3-4 minutes or until desired doneness, flipping once.

5. Meanwhile, for green beans: in a pan of boiling water, arrange a steamer basket.

6. Place the green beans in steamer basket and steam covered for about 4-5 minutes.

7. Carefully transfer the beans into a bowl.

8. Add olive oil and lemon juice and toss to coat well.

9. Divide green beans onto serving plates.

10. Top each with 1 steak and serve.

Beef with Mushrooms

Servings: 4

Preparation Time: 15 minutes

Cooking Time: 15 minutes

Ingredients:

For Beef:

- 4 (6-ounce) beef tenderloin fillets
- Salt and freshly ground black pepper, to taste
- 2 tablespoons olive oil, divided
- 1 teaspoon garlic, smashed
- 1 tablespoon fresh thyme, chopped

For Mushrooms:

- 2 tablespoons olive oil
- 1-pound fresh mushrooms, sliced
- 2 teaspoons garlic, smashed
- Salt and freshly ground black pepper, to taste

Directions:

1. For beef: season the beef fillets with salt and black pepper evenly and set aside.

2. In a cast-iron skillet, heat the oil over medium heat and sauté the garlic and thyme for about 1 minute.

3. Add the fillets and cook for about 5-7 minutes per side.

4. Meanwhile, for mushrooms: in another cast-iron skillet, heat the oil over medium heat and cook the mushrooms, garlic, salt, and black pepper for about 7-8 minutes, stirring frequently.

5. Divide the fillets onto serving plates.

6. Top with mushroom mixture and serve.

Steak with Carrot & Kale

Servings: 4

Preparation Time: 15 minutes

Cooking Time: 12 minutes

Ingredients:

*   2 tablespoons olive oil
*   4 garlic cloves, minced
*   1-pound beef sirloin steak, cut into bite-sized pieces Freshly ground black pepper, to taste
*   1½ cups carrots, peeled and cut into matchsticks
*   1½ cups fresh kale, tough ribs removed and chopped
*   3 tablespoons low-sodium soy sauce

Directions:

1. In a skillet, heat the oil over medium heat and sauté the garlic for about 1 minute.

2. Add the beef and black pepper and stir to combine.

3. Increase the heat to medium-high and cook for about 3-4 minutes or until browned from all sides.

4. Add the carrot, kale and soy sauce and cook for about 4-5 minutes.

5. Stir in the black pepper and remove from the heat.

6. Serve hot

Lemon Beef

Servings: 4

Preparation Time: 10 minutes.

Cooking Time: 6 hours.

Ingredients:

*   1 lb beef chuck roast.
*   1 fresh lime juice.
*   1 garlic clove, crushed.
*   1 teaspoon chili powder.
*   2 cups lemon-lime soda.

*   1/2 teaspoon salt.

Directions:

1.   Place beef chuck roast into the slow cooker.

2.   Season roast with garlic, chili powder, and salt.

3.   Pour lemon-lime soda over the roast.

4.   Cover slow cooker and cook on low for 6 hours. Shred the meat using a fork.

5.   Add lime juice over shredded roast and serve.

Veggie & Feta Stuffed Steak

Servings: 6

Preparation Time: 15 minutes

Cooking Time: 35 minutes

Ingredients:

*   12 tablespoons dried oregano leaves 1/3 cup fresh lemon juice
*   2 tablespoons olive oil
*   1 (2-pound) beef flank steak, pounded into ½-inch thickness. 1/3 cup olive tapenade
*   1 cup frozen chopped spinach, thawed and squeezed ¼ cup feta cheese, crumbled
*   4 cups fresh cherry tomatoes Salt, as required

Directions:

1. In a large baking dish, add the oregano, lemon juice and oil and mix well.

2. Add the steak and coat with the marinade generously.

3. Refrigerate to marinate for about 4 hours, flipping occasionally.

4. Preheat the oven to 425 degrees F.

5. Line a shallow baking dish with parchment paper.

6. Remove the steak from baking dish, reserving the remaining marinade in a bowl.

7. Cover the bowl of marinade and refrigerate.

8. Arrange the steak onto a cutting board.

9. Place the tapenade onto the steak evenly and top with the spinach, followed by the feta cheese.

10. Carefully roll the steak tightly to form a log.

11. With 6 kitchen string pieces, tie the log at 6 places.

12. Carefully cut the log between strings into 6 equal pieces, leaving string in place.

13. In a bowl, add the reserved marinade, tomatoes and salt and toss to coat.

14. Arrange the log pieces onto the prepared baking dish, cut-side up.

15. Now, arrange the tomatoes around the pinwheels evenly.

16. Bake for approximately 25-35 minutes.

17. Remove from the oven and set aside for about 5 minutes before serving.

Salmon with Cauliflower Mash

Servings: 4

Preparation Time: 15 minutes

Cooking Time: 20 minutes

Ingredients:

For Cauliflower Mash:

- 1-pound cauliflower, cut into florets
- 1 tablespoon extra-virgin olive oil
- 3 garlic cloves, minced
- 1 teaspoon fresh thyme leaves
- Salt and freshly ground black pepper, to taste

For Salmon:

- 1 (1-inch) piece fresh ginger, grated finely
- 1 tablespoon honey
- 1 tablespoon fresh lemon juice
- 1 tablespoon Dijon mustard
- 2 tablespoons olive oil
- 4 (6-ounce) salmon fillets
- 2 tablespoons fresh parsley, chopped

Directions:

1. For mash: in a large saucepan of water, arrange a steamer basket and bring to a boil.

2. Place the cauliflower florets in steamer basket and steam covered for about 10 minutes.

3. Drain the cauliflower and set aside.

4. In a small frying pan, heat the oil over medium heat and sauté the garlic for about 2 minutes.

5. Remove the frying pan from heat and transfer the garlic oil in a large food processor.

6. Add the cauliflower, thyme, salt and black pepper and pulse until smooth.

7. Transfer the cauliflower mash into a bowl and set aside.

8. Meanwhile, in a bowl, mix together ginger, honey, lemon juice and Dijon mustard. Set aside.

9. In a large non-stick skillet, heat olive oil over medium-high heat and cook the salmon fillets for about 3-4 minutes per side.

10. Stir in honey mixture and immediately remove from heat.

11. Divide warm cauliflower mash onto serving plates.

12. Top each plate with 1 salmon fillet and serve.

Moroccan Meatballs

Servings: 5

Preparation Time: 10 Minutes.

Cooking Time: 20 Minutes.

Ingredients:

- ¼ cup finely chopped onion (about ⅛ onion).
- ¼ cup raisins, coarsely chopped.
- 1 teaspoon ground cumin.
- ½ teaspoon ground cinnamon.
- ¼ teaspoon smoked paprika.
- 1 large egg.
- 1 pound ground beef (93% lean) or ground lamb.
- ⅓ cup panko bread crumbs.
- 1 teaspoon extra-virgin olive oil.
- 1 (28-ounce) can low-sodium or no-salt-added crushed tomatoes Chopped fresh mint, feta cheese, and/or
- fresh orange or lemon wedges, for serving.

Directions:

1. In a large bowl, combine the onion, raisins, cumin, cinnamon, smoked paprika, and egg. Add the groundbeef and bread crumbs and mix gently with your hands. Divide the mixture into 20 even portions, then wet your hands and roll each portion into a ball. Wash your hands.

2. In a large skillet over medium-high heat, heat the oil. Add the meatballs and cook for 8 minutes, rolling around every minute or so with tongs or a fork to brown them on most sides. (They won't be cooked through.) Transfer the meatballs to a paper towel-lined plate. Drain the fat out of the pan, and carefully wipe out the hot pan with a paper towel.

3. Return the meatballs to the pan, and pour the tomatoes over the meatballs. Cover and

cook on medium-high heat until the sauce begins to bubble. Lower the heat to medium, cover partially, and cook for 7 to 8 more minutes, until the meatballs are cooked through. Garnish with fresh mint, feta cheese, and/or a squeeze of citrus, if desired, and serve.

Beef Spanakopita Pita Pockets

Servings: 5

Preparation Time: 5 Minutes.

Cooking Time: 15 Minutes.

Ingredients:

- 3 teaspoons extra-virgin olive oil, divided.
- 1 pound ground beef (93% lean).
- 2 garlic cloves, minced.
- 2 (6-ounce) bags baby spinach, chopped.
- ½ cup crumbled feta cheese (about 2 ounces).
- ⅓ cup ricotta cheese.
- ½ teaspoon ground nutmeg.
- ¼ teaspoon freshly ground black pepper.
- ¼ cup slivered almonds.
- 4 (6-inch) whole-wheat pita breads, cut in half.

Directions:

1. In a large skillet over medium heat, heat 1 teaspoon of oil. Add the ground beef and cook for 10 minutes, breaking it up with a wooden spoon and stirring occasionally. Remove from the heat and drain in a colander. Set the meat aside.

2. Place the skillet back on the heat, and add the remaining 2 teaspoons of oil. Add the garlic and cook for 1 minute, stirring constantly. Add the spinach and cook for 2 to 3 minutes, or until the spinach has cooked down, stirring often.

3. Turn off the heat and mix in the feta cheese, ricotta, nutmeg, and pepper. Stir until all the ingredients arewell incorporated. Mix in the almonds.

4. Divide the beef filling among the eight pita pocket halves to stuff them and serve.

Pork Cacciatore

Servings: 5

Preparation Time: 15 Minutes.

Cooking Time: 6 hours.

Ingredients:

- 1 ½ lbs. pork chops.
- 1 teaspoon dried oregano.
- 1 cup beef broth.
- 3 tablespoon tomato paste.
- 14 oz. can tomatoes, diced.
- 2 cups mushrooms, sliced.
- 1 small onion, diced.
- 1 garlic clove, minced.
- 2 tablespoon olive oil.
- ¼ teaspoon pepper.
- ½ teaspoon salt.

Directions:

1. Heat oil in a pan over medium heat.

2. Add pork chops in a pan and cook until brown on both sides.

3. Transfer pork chops into the crockpot.

4. Pour remaining ingredients over the pork chops.

5. Cover and cook on low heat for 6 hours.

6. Serve and enjoy.

Mini Greek Meatloaves

Servings: 5

Preparation Time: 5 Minutes.

Cooking Time: 25 Minutes.

Ingredients:

- Non-stick cooking spray.
- 1 tablespoon extra-virgin olive oil.
- ½ cup minced onion (about ¼ onion).
- 1 garlic clove, minced (about ½ teaspoon).
- 1 pound ground beef (93% lean).
- ½ cup whole-wheat bread crumbs.
- ½ cup crumbled feta cheese (about 2 ounces).
- 1 large egg.
- ½ teaspoon dried oregano, crushed between your fingers.
- ¼ teaspoon freshly ground black pepper.
- ½ cup 2% plain Greek yogurt.
- ⅓ cup chopped and pitted Kalamata olives.
- 2 tablespoons olive brine.
- Romaine lettuce or pita bread, for serving (optional).

Directions:

1.   Preheat the oven to 400°F. Coat a 12-cup muffin pan with non-stick cooking spray and set aside.

2.   In a small skillet over medium heat, heat the oil. Add the onion and cook for 4 minutes, stirring frequently.

3.   Add the garlic and cook for 1 more minute, stirring frequently. Remove from the heat.

4.   In a large mixing bowl, combine the onion and garlic with the ground beef, bread crumbs, feta, egg, oregano, and pepper. Gently mix together with your hands.

5.   Divide into 12 portions and place in the muffin cups. Cook for 18 to 20 minutes, or until the internal temperature of the meat is 160°F on a meat thermometer.

6.   While the meatloaves are baking, in a small bowl, whisk together the yogurt, olives, and olive brine.

7.   When you're ready to serve, place the meatloaves on a serving platter and spoon the olive-yogurt sauce on top. You can also serve them on a bed of lettuce or with cut-up pieces of pita bread.

Smoky Pork & Cabbage

Servings: 5
Preparation Time: 15 Minutes.
Cooking Time: 8 hours.
Ingredients:
* 3 lbs. pork roast.
* 1/2 cabbage head, chopped.
* 1 cup water.
* 1/3 cup liquid smoke.
* 1 tablespoon kosher salt.

Directions:
1.   Rub pork with kosher salt and place into the crockpot.

2.   Pour liquid smoke over the pork. Add water.

3.   Cover and cook on low heat for 7 hours.

4.   Remove pork from the crockpot and add cabbage to the bottom of the crockpot.

5.   Place pork on top of the cabbage.

6.   Cover again and cook for 1 more hour.

7.   Shred pork with a fork and serves.

Halibut with Zucchini

Servings: 4
Preparation Time: 15 minutes
Cooking Time: 20 minutes
Ingredients:
* 1 teaspoon olive oil
* ½ cup yellow onion, minced
* 1 cup zucchini, chopped
* 2 garlic cloves, minced
* 2 tablespoons fresh basil, chopped
* 2 cups fresh tomatoes, chopped
* Salt and freshly ground black pepper, to taste
* 4 (6-ounce) halibut steaks
* 1/3 cup feta cheese, crumbled

Directions:
1. Preheat your oven to 450 degrees F.

2. Grease a large shallow baking dish.

3. In a skillet, heat the oil over medium heat and sauté the onion, zucchini and garlic for about 4-5 minutes.

4. Stir in the basil, tomatoes and black pepper and immediately remove from heat.

5. Place the halibut steaks into the prepared baking dish in a single layer.

6. Top with the tomato mixture evenly and sprinkle with cheese evenly.

7. Bake for approximately 15 minutes or until desired doneness.

8. Serve hot.

Pork Roast

Servings: 5
Preparation Time: 15 Minutes.
Cooking Time: 1 hour.
Ingredients:
* 3 lbs. pork roast, boneless.
* 1 cup water.
* 1 onion, chopped.
* 3 garlic cloves, chopped.
* 1 tablespoon black pepper.
* 1 rosemary sprig.
* 2 fresh oregano sprigs.
* 2 fresh thyme sprigs.
* 1 tablespoon olive oil.

- 1 tablespoon kosher salt.

Directions:

1. Preheat the oven to 350°F.

2. Season pork roast with pepper and salt.

3. Add onion and garlic. Pour in the water, oregano, and thyme and bring to boil for a minute.

4. Cover pot and roast in the preheated oven for 1 1/2 hours.

5. Serve and enjoy.

Salmon with Asparagus

Servings: 6

Preparation Time: 10 minutes

Cooking Time: 20 minutes

Ingredients:

- 6 (4-ounce) salmon fillets
- 2 tablespoons extra-virgin olive oil
- 3 tablespoons fresh parsley, minced ¼ teaspoon ginger powder
- Salt and freshly ground black pepper, to taste 1½ pounds fresh asparagus

Directions:

1. Preheat your oven to 400 degrees.

2. Grease a large baking dish.

3. In a bowl, place all ingredients and mix well.

4. Arrange the salmon fillets into prepared baking dish in a single layer.

5. Bake for approximately 15-20 minutes or until desired doneness of salmon.

6. Meanwhile, in a pan of the boiling water, add asparagus and cook for about 4-5 minutes.

7. Drain the asparagus well.

8. Divide the asparagus onto serving plates evenly and top each with 1 salmon fillet and serve.

Pork Stuffed Avocado

Servings: 8

Preparation Time: 15 minutes

Cooking Time: 10 minutes

Ingredients:

- 4 ripe avocados, halved and pitted
- 3 tablespoons fresh lime juice
- 1 tablespoon olive oil
- 1 medium onion, chopped

- 1-pound ground pork
- 1 packet taco seasoning
- Salt and ground black pepper, as required
- 2/3 cup low-fat Mexican cheese, shredded
- ½ cup lettuce, shredded
- ½ cup cherry tomatoes, quartered

Directions:

1. Carefully remove abut about 2-3 tablespoons of flesh from each avocado half.

2. Chop the avocado flesh and reserve it.

3. Arrange the avocado halves onto a tray and drizzle each with lime juice.

4. In a medium skillet, heat oil over medium heat and sauté the onion for about 5 minutes.

5. Add the ground pork, taco seasoning, salt and black pepper and cook for about 8-10 minutes, breaking up the meat with a wooden spoon.

6. Remove from the heat and drain the grease from the skillet.

7. Stuff each avocado half with pork and top with reserved avocado, cheese, lettuce and tomato.

8. Serve immediately.

Salmon Lettuce Wraps

Servings: 2

Preparation Time: 10 minutes

Ingredients:

- ¼ cup low-fat mozzarella cheese, cubed ¼ cup tomato, chopped
- 2 tablespoons fresh dill, chopped
- 1 teaspoon fresh lemon juice Salt, as required
- 4 lettuce leaves
- 1/3 pound cooked salmon, chopped

Directions:

1. In a small bowl, combine mozzarella, tomato, dill, lemon juice, and salt until well combined.

2. Arrange the lettuce leaves onto serving plates.

3. Divide the salmon and tomato mixture over each lettuce leaf and serve immediately.

Tuna Burgers

Servings: 2
Preparation Time: 15 minutes
Cooking Time: 6 minutes
Ingredients:

- 1 (15-ounce) can water-packed tuna, drained ½ celery stalk, chopped
- 2 tablespoon fresh parsley, chopped
- 1 teaspoon fresh dill, chopped
- 2 tablespoon walnuts, chopped
- 2 tablespoon mayonnaise
- 1 egg, beaten
- 1 tablespoon butter
- 3 cups lettuce

Directions:

1. For Burgers: add all ingredients except the butter and lettuce in a bowl and mix until well combined.
2. Make 2 equal-sized patties from mixture.
3. In a frying pan, melt butter over medium heat and cook the patties for about 2-3 minutes.
4. Carefully flip the side and cook for about 2-3 minutes.
5. Divide the lettuce onto serving plates.
6. Top each plate with 1 burger and serve.

Spicy Salmon

Servings: 4
Preparation Time: 105 minutes
Cooking Time: 8 minutes
Ingredients:

- 4 tablespoons extra-virgin olive oil, divided
- 2 tablespoons fresh lemon juice
- 1 teaspoon ground turmeric
- 1 teaspoon ground cumin
- Salt and ground black pepper, as required
- 4 (4-ounce) boneless, skinless salmon fillets
- 6 cups fresh arugula

Directions:

1. In a bowl, mix together 2 tablespoons of oil, lemon juice, turmeric, cumin, salt and black pepper.
2. Add the salmon fillets and coat with the oil mixture generously. Set aside.
3. In a non-stick wok, heat remaining oil over medium heat.
4. Place salmon fillets, skin-side down and cook for about 3-5 minutes.
5. Change the side and cook for about 2-3 minutes more.
6. Divide the salmon onto serving plates and serve immediately alongside the arugula.

Salmon with Salsa

Servings: 4
Preparation Time: 15 minutes
Cooking Time: 8 minutes
Ingredients:
For Salsa:

- 2 large ripe avocados, peeled, pitted and cut into small chunks
- 1 small tomato, chopped
- 2 tablespoons red onion, chopped finely
- ¼ cup fresh cilantro, chopped finely
- 1 tablespoon jalapeño pepper, seeded and minced finely
- 1 garlic clove, minced finely
- 3 tablespoon fresh lime juice
- Salt and ground black pepper, as required

For Salmon:

- 4 (5-ounce) (1-inch thick) salmon fillets
- Sea salt and ground black pepper, as required
- 3 tablespoons olive oil
- 1 tablespoon fresh rosemary leaves, chopped
- 1 tablespoon fresh lemon juice

Directions:

1. For salsa: add all ingredients in a bowl and gently, stir to combine.
2. With a plastic wrap, cover the bowl and refrigerate before serving.
3. For salmon: season each salmon fillet with salt and black pepper generously.
4. In a large skillet, heat the oil over medium-high heat.
5. Place the salmon fillets, skins side up and cook for about 4 minutes.
6. Carefully change the side of each salmon fillet and cook for about 4 minutes more.
7. Stir in the rosemary and lemon juice and remove from the heat.
8. Divide the salsa onto serving plates evenly.

9. To each plate with 1 salmon fillet and serve.

Shrimp with Broccoli & Carrot

Servings: 5

Preparation Time: 15 minutes

Cooking Time: 8 minutes

Ingredients:

For Sauce:

- 1 tablespoon fresh ginger, grated
- 2 garlic cloves, minced
- 3 tablespoons low-sodium soy sauce
- 1 tablespoon balsamic vinegar
- 1 teaspoon Erythritol
- ¼ teaspoon red pepper flakes, crushed

For Shrimp Mixture:

- 3 tablespoons olive oil
- 1½ pounds medium shrimp, peeled and deveined
- 12 ounces broccoli florets
- 8 ounces, carrot, peeled and sliced

Directions:

1. For sauce: in a bow, place all the ingredients and beat until well combined. Set aside.

2. In a large wok, heat oil over medium-high heat and cook the shrimp for about 2 minutes, stirring occasionally.

3. Add the broccoli and carrot and cook about 3-4 minutes, stirring frequently.

4. Stir in the sauce mixture and cook for about 1-2 minutes.

Lemon Pepper Pork Tenderloin

Servings: 5

Preparation Time: 15 Minutes.

Cooking Time: 25 Minutes.

Ingredients:

- 1 lb. pork tenderloin.
- 3/4 teaspoon lemon pepper.
- 3 teaspoon dried oregano.
- 1 tablespoon olive oil.
- 3 tablespoon feta cheese, crumbled.
- 3 tablespoon olive tapenades.

Directions:

1. Add pork, oil, lemon pepper, and oregano in a zip-lock bag and rub well and place in a refrigerator for 2 hours.

2. Remove pork from zip-lock bag. Using a sharp knife, make a lengthwise cut through the center of the tenderloin.

3. Spread olive tapenade on half tenderloin and sprinkle with feta cheese.

4. Fold another half of the meat over to the original shape of the tenderloin.

5. Tie close pork tenderloin with twine at 2-inch intervals.

6. Grill pork tenderloin for 20 minutes.

7. Cut into slices and serve.

Roasted Mackerel

Servings: 2

Preparation Time: 10 minutes

Cooking Time: 20 minutes

Ingredients:

- 2 (7-ounce) mackerel fillets
- 1 tablespoon olive oil
- Salt and ground black pepper, to taste
- 3 cups fresh baby greens

Directions:

1. Preheat your oven to 350 degree F.

2. Arrange a rack in the middle of oven.

3. Lightly grease a baking dish.

4. Brush the fish fillets with melted butter and then season with salt and black pepper.

5. Arrange the fish fillets into the prepared baking dish in a single layer.

6. Bake for approximately 20 minutes.

7. Serve hot alongside the greens.

Shrimp with Zucchini Noodles

Servings: 4

Preparation Time: 20 minutes

Cooking Time: 8 minutes

Ingredients:

- 2 tablespoons olive oil
- 1 garlic clove, minced
- ¼ teaspoon red pepper flakes, crushed
- 1-pound shrimp, peeled and deveined
- Salt and ground black pepper, as required
  1/3 cup low-sodium chicken broth
- 2 medium zucchinis, spiralized with blade C
- 1 cup cherry tomatoes, quartered

Directions:

1. In a large non-stick skillet, heat the olive oil over medium heat and sauté garlic and red pepper flakes for about 1 minute.

2. Add the shrimp, salt and black pepper and cook for about 1 minute per side.

3. Add the broth and zucchini noodles and cook for about 3-4 minutes.

4. Stir in the tomato quarters and remove from the heat.

5. Serve hot.

Herbed Sea Bass

Servings: 2

Preparation Time: 10 minutes

Cooking Time: 20 minutes

Ingredients:

* 2 (1¼-pound) whole sea bass, gutted, gilled, scaled and fins removed Salt and ground black pepper, as required
* 6 fresh bay leaves
* 2 fresh thyme sprigs
* 2 fresh parsley sprigs
* 2 fresh rosemary sprigs
* 2 tablespoons butter, melted
* 2 tablespoons fresh lemon juice
* 3 cups fresh arugula

Directions:

1. Season the cavity and outer side of each fish with salt and black pepper evenly.

2. With a plastic wrap, cover each fish and refrigerate for 1 hour.

3. Preheat the oven to 450 degrees F.

4. Lightly grease a baking dish.

5. Arrange 2 bay leaves in the bottom of prepared baking dish.

6. Divide herb sprigs and remaining bay leaves inside the cavity of each fish.

7. Arrange both fish over bay leave in baking dish and drizzle with butter.

8. Roast for about 15-20 minutes or until fish is cooked through.

9. Remove the baking dish from oven and place the fish onto a platter.

10. Drizzle the fish with lemon juice and serve alongside the arugula.

Lemony Trout

Servings: 4

Preparation Time: 15 minutes

Cooking Time: 25 minutes

Ingredients:

* 2 (1½-pound) wild-caught trout, gutted and cleaned Salt and ground black pepper, as required
* 1 lemon, sliced
* 2 tablespoons fresh dill, minced
* 2 tablespoons butter, melted
* 2 tablespoons fresh lemon juice

Directions:

1. Preheat the oven to 475 degrees F.

2. Arrange a wire rack onto a foil-lined baking sheet.

3. Sprinkle the trout with salt and black pepper from inside and outside generously.

4. Fill the cavity of each fish with lemon slices and dill.

5. Place the trout onto prepared baking sheet and drizzle with the melted butter and lemon juice.

6. Bake for approximately 25 minutes.

7. Remove the baking sheet from oven and transfer the trout onto a serving platter.

8. Serve hot.

Tuna Stuffed Avocado

Servings: 2

Preparation Time: 15 minutes

Ingredients:

* 1 large avocado, halved and pitted
* 1 tablespoon onion, chopped finely
* 2 tablespoons fresh lemon juice
* 5 ounces cooked tuna, chopped
* Salt and ground black pepper, as required

Directions:

1. With a spoon, scoop out the flesh from the middle of each avocado half and transfer into a bowl.

2. Add the onion and lemon juice and mash until well combined.

3. Add tuna, salt and black pepper and stir to combine.

4. Divide the tuna mixture in both avocado halves evenly and serve immediately.

Fish & Spinach Curry

Servings: 4

Preparation Time: 15 minutes

Cooking Time: 15 minutes

Ingredients:

- 1 tablespoon coconut oil
- 1 small yellow onion, chopped
- 2 garlic cloves, minced
- 1 teaspoon fresh ginger, minced
- 1 large tomato, peeled and chopped
- 1 tablespoon curry powder
- ¼ cup water
- 1¼ cups unsweetened coconut milk
- 1-pound skinless grouper fillets, cubed into 2-inch size ¾ pound fresh spinach, chopped
- Salt, as required
- 2 tablespoons fresh parsley, chopped

Directions:

1. In a large wok, melt the coconut oil over medium heat and sauté the onion, garlic and ginger for about 5 minutes.

2. Add the tomatoes and curry powder and cook for about 2-3 minutes, crushing with the back of spoon.

3. Add the water and coconut milk and bring to a gentle boil.

4. Stir in grouper pieces and spinach and cook for about 4-5 minutes.

5. Stir in the salt and parsley and serve hot.

Shrimp with Spinach

Servings: 4

Preparation Time: 15 minutes

Cooking Time: 9 minutes

Ingredients:

- 3 tablespoons extra-virgin olive oil
- 1-pound medium shrimp, peeled and deveined
- 1 medium onion, chopped
- 2 garlic cloves, chopped finely
- 1 fresh red chili, sliced
- 1-pound fresh spinach, chopped
- ¼ cup low-sodium chicken broth

Directions:

1. In a large non-stick skillet, heat 1 tablespoon of the oil over medium-high heat and cook the shrimp for about 2 minutes per side.

2. With a slotted spoon, transfer the shrimp onto a plate.

3. In the same skillet, heat the remaining 2 tablespoons of oil over medium heat and sauté the garlic and red chili for about 1 minute.

4. Add the spinach and broth and cook for about 2-3 minutes, stirring occasionally.

5. Stir in the cooked shrimp and cook for about 1 minute.

6. Serve hot.

Salmon Cakes

Servings: 2

Preparation Time: 10 Minutes.

Cooking Time: 10 Minutes.

Ingredients:

- 2 cans salmon (14.75 ounces each), drained.
- 8 tablespoons collagen.
- 2 cups shredded mozzarella cheese.
- 1 teaspoon onion powder.
- 4 large pastured eggs.
- 4 teaspoons dried dill.
- 1 teaspoon pink sea salt or to taste.
- 4 tablespoons bacon grease.

Directions:

1. Add salmon, collagen, mozzarella, onion powder, eggs, dill, and salt into a bowl and mix well.

2. Make 8 patties from the mixture.

3. Place a large skillet over a medium-low flame with bacon grease. Once the fat is well heated, place the salmon cakes in the skillet and cook until it becomes golden brown on all sides.

4. Take off the pan from heat and let the patties remain in the cooked fat for 5 minutes. Serve.

Fish Bone Broth

Servings: 2

Preparation Time: 10 Minutes.

Cooking Time: 10 minutes.

Ingredients:

- 2 pounds of fish head or carcass.

- Salt to taste.
- 7–8 quarts water + extra to blanch.
- 2 inches ginger, sliced.
- 2 tablespoons lemon juice.

Directions:

1. To blanch the fish: Add water and fish heads into a large pot. Place the pot over high heat.

2. When it boils, turn the heat off and discard the water.

3. Place the fish back in the pot. Pour 7–8 quarts of water.

4. Place the pot over high heat. Add ginger, salt, and lemon juice.

5. When the mixture boils, reduce the heat and cover with a lid. Simmer for 4 hours.

6. Remove from heat. When it cools down, strain into a large jar with a wire mesh strainer.

7. Refrigerate for 5–6 days. Unused broth can be frozen.

Cauliflower with Peas

Servings: 4

Preparation Time: 15 minutes

Cooking Time: 15 minutes

Ingredients:

- 2 medium tomatoes, chopped
- ¼ cup water
- 2 tablespoons olive oil
- 3 garlic cloves, minced
- ½ tablespoon fresh ginger, minced
- 1 teaspoon ground cumin
- 2 teaspoons ground coriander
- 1 teaspoon cayenne pepper
- ¼ teaspoon ground turmeric
- 2 cups cauliflower, chopped
- 1 cup fresh green peas, shelled
- Salt and ground black pepper, as required ½ cup warm water

Directions:

1. In a blender, add tomato and ¼ cup of water and pulse until a smooth puree forms. Set aside.

2. In a large skillet, heat the oil over medium heat and sauté the garlic, ginger, green chilies and spices for about 1 minute.

3. Add the cauliflower, peas and tomato puree and cook, stirring for about 3-4 minutes.

4. Add the warm water and bring to a boil.

5. Reduce the heat to medium-low and cook, covered for about 8-10 minutes or until vegetables are done completely.

6. Serve hot.

Prawns with Asparagus

Servings: 4

Preparation Time: 15 minutes

Cooking Time: 13 minutes

Ingredients:

- 3 tablespoons extra-virgin olive oil
- 1-pound prawns, peeled and deveined 1-pound asparagus, trimmed
- Salt and ground black pepper, as required
- 1 teaspoon garlic, minced
- 1 teaspoon fresh ginger, minced
- 1 tablespoon low-sodium soy sauce
- 2 tablespoons lemon juice

Directions:

1. In a wok, heat 2 tablespoons of oil over medium-high heat and cook the prawns with salt and black pepper for about 3-4 minutes.

2. With a slotted spoon, transfer the prawns into a bowl. Set aside.

3. In the same wok, heat remaining 1 tablespoon of oil over medium-high heat and cook the asparagus,ginger, garlic, salt and black pepper and for about 6-8 minutes, stirring frequently.

4. Stir in the prawns and soy sauce and cook for about 1 minute.

5. Stir in the lemon juice and remove from the heat.

6. Serve hot.

Garlic Butter Shrimp

Servings: 2

Preparation Time: 10 Minutes.

Cooking Time: 10 Minutes.

Ingredients:

1 cup unsalted butter, divided.

Kosher salt to taste.

½ cup chicken stock.

Freshly ground pepper to taste.

¼ cup chopped fresh parsley leaves.

3 pounds medium shrimp, peeled, deveined.

Garlic.

Juice of 2 lemons.

Directions:

1.   Add 4 tablespoons butter into a large skillet and place the skillet over medium-high flame. Once butter melts, stir in salt, shrimp, and pepper and cook for 2–3 minutes. Stir every minute or so. Remove shrimp with a slotted spoon and place on a plate.

2.   Add garlic into the pot and cook until you get a nice aroma. Pour lemon juice and stock and stir.

3.   Once it comes to a boil, lower the heat and cook until the stock reduces to half its initial quantity.

4.   Add the rest of the butter, a tablespoon each time, and stir until it melts each time.

5.   Add shrimp and stir lightly until well coated.

6.   Sprinkle parsley on top and serve.

Tofu with Kale

Servings: 2

Preparation Time: 15 minutes

Cooking Time: 10 minutes

Ingredients:

- 1 tablespoon extra-virgin olive oil
- ½ pound tofu, pressed, drained and cubed
- 1 teaspoon fresh ginger, minced
- 1 garlic clove, minced
- ¼ teaspoon red pepper flakes, crushed
- 6 ounces fresh kale, tough ribs removed and chopped finely
- 1 tablespoon low-sodium soy sauce

Directions:

1. In a large non-stick wok, heat olive oil over medium-high heat and stir-fry the tofu for about 3-3 minutes.

2. Add the ginger, garlic and red pepper flakes and cook for about 1 minute, stirring continuously.

3. Stir in the kale and soy sauce and stir-fry for about 4-5 minutes.

4. Serve hot.

Bok Choy & Mushroom Stir Fry

Servings: 4

Preparation Time: 15 minutes

Cooking Time: 10 minutes

Ingredients:

- 1-pound baby bok choy
- 4 teaspoons olive oil
- 1 teaspoon fresh ginger, minced
- 2 garlic cloves, chopped
- 5 ounces fresh mushrooms, sliced
- 2 tablespoons red wine
- 2 tablespoons soy sauce
- Ground black pepper, as required

Directions:

1. Trim bases of bok choy and separate outer leaves from stalks, leaving the smallest inner leaves attached.

2. In a large cast-iron wok, heat the oil over medium-high heat and sauté the ginger and garlic for about 1 minute.

3. Stir in the mushrooms and cook for about 4-5 minutes, stirring frequently.

4. Stir in the bok choy leaves and stalks and cook for about 1 minute, tossing with tongs.

5. Stir in the wine, soy sauce and black pepper and cook for about 2-3 minutes, tossing occasionally.

6. Serve hot.

Grilled Shrimp

Servings: 2

Preparation Time: 10 Minutes.

Cooking Time: 5 Minutes.

Ingredients:

- 2 teaspoons garlic powder.
- 2 teaspoons Italian seasoning.
- 2 teaspoons kosher salt.
- ½ - 1 teaspoon cayenne pepper.

Grilling:

- 4 tablespoons extra-virgin olive oil.
- 2 pounds shrimp, peeled, deveined.
- 2 tablespoons fresh lemon juice.
- Oil to grease the grill grated.

Directions:

1.   You can grill the shrimp in a grill or boil it in an oven. Choose whatever method suits you and preheat thegrill or oven to high heat.

2.   In case you are broiling it in an oven, prepare a baking sheet by lining it with foil and greasing the foil as well, with some fat.

3.   Add garlic powder, cayenne pepper, salt, and Italian seasoning into a large bowl and mix well.

4.   Add lemon juice and oil and mix well.

5.   Stir in the shrimp. Make sure that the shrimp are well coated with the mixture.

6.   If using the grill, fix the shrimp on skewers else, place them on the baking sheet.

7.   Grease the grill grates with some oil. Grill the shrimp or broil them in an oven until they turn pink. It shoul take 2–3 minutes for each side.

Stuffed Zucchini

Servings: 8

Preparation Time: 15 minutes

Cooking Time: 18 minutes

Ingredients:

- 4 medium zucchinis, halved lengthwise
- 1 cup red bell pepper, seeded and minced ½ cup Kalamata olives, pitted and minced ½ cup tomatoes, minced
- 1 teaspoon garlic, minced
- 1 tablespoon dried oregano, crushed
- Salt and ground black pepper, as required ½ cup feta cheese, crumbled
- ¼ cup fresh parsley, chopped finely

Directions:

1. Preheat your oven to 350 degrees F.

2. Grease a large baking sheet.

3. With a melon baller, scoop out the flesh of each zucchini half. Discard the flesh.

4. In a bowl, mix together bell pepper, olives, tomato, garlic, oregano and black pepper.

5. Stuff each zucchini half with veggie mixture evenly.

6. Arrange zucchini halves onto prepared baking sheet and Bake for approximately 15 minutes.

7. Now, set the oven to broiler on high.

8. Top each zucchini half with feta cheese and broil for about 3 minutes.

9. Garnish with parsley and serve hot.

Tempeh with Veggies

Servings: 3

Preparation Time: 15 minutes

Cooking Time: 17 minutes

Ingredients:

For Sauce:

- 3 tablespoons tahini
- 2 tablespoons low-sodium soy sauce
- 1 tablespoon sesame oil
- 1 tablespoon chili garlic sauce
- 1 tablespoon maple syrup

For tempeh & Veggies:

- 3 tablespoons olive oil, divided
- 8 ounces tempeh, cut into 1x2-inch rectangular strips
- 8 ounces fresh button mushrooms, sliced thinly
- 8 ounces fresh spinach
- 1 tablespoon fresh ginger, minced
- 1 tablespoon garlic, minced

Directions:

1. For sauce: in a bowl, add all ingredients and beat until well combined.

2. In a large skillet, heat the oil over medium-high heat and cook the tempeh for about 4-5 minutes or until browned.

3. With a slotted spoon, transfer the tempeh into a bowl and set aside.

4. In the same skillet, heat the remaining oil over medium-high heat and cook the mushrooms for about 6-

7 minutes, stirring frequently.

5. With a slotted spoon, transfer the mushrooms into a bowl and set aside.

6. In the same skillet, add the spinach, ginger and garlic and cook for about 2-3 minutes.

7. Stir in the cooked tempeh, mushrooms and sauce and cook for about 1-2 minutes, stirring continuously.

8. Serve hot.

Prawns with Bell Pepper

Servings: 4

Preparation Time: 20 minutes

Cooking Time: 8 minutes

Ingredients:

- 2 tablespoons olive oil
- 4 garlic cloves, minced
- 1 fresh red chili, sliced
- 1-pound prawns, peeled and deveined

- ½ cup green bell pepper, seeded and julienned
- ½ cup yellow bell pepper, seeded and julienned
- ½ cup red bell pepper, seeded and julienned
- ½ cup orange bell pepper, seeded and julienned
- ½ cup white onion, sliced thinly
- ¼ cup low-sodium chicken broth
- Salt and ground black pepper, as required

Directions:

1. In a large non-stick skillet, heat olive oil over medium heat and sauté the garlic and red chili for about 2 minutes.

2. Add the prawn, bell peppers, onion and black pepper and stir fry for about 5 minutes.

3. Stir in the broth and cook for about 1 minute.

4. Serve hot.

Shrimp & Scallops with Veggies

Servings: 5

Preparation Time: 20 minutes

Cooking Time: 11 minutes

Ingredients:

- 3 tablespoons olive oil, divided
- 1-pound fresh asparagus, cut into 2-inch pieces
- 2 red bell peppers, seeded and chopped
- ¾ pound medium raw shrimp, peeled and deveined ¾ pound raw scallops
- 1 tablespoon dried parsley
- ½ teaspoon garlic, minced
- Salt and freshly ground black pepper, to taste

Directions:

1. In a large skillet, heat 1 tablespoon of oil over medium heat and stir-fry the asparagus and bell peppers for about 4-5 minutes.

2. With a slotted spoon, transfer the vegetables onto a plate.

3. In the same skillet, heat the remaining oil over medium heat and stir-fry shrimp and scallops for about 2 minutes.

4. Stir in the parsley, garlic, salt, and black pepper, and cook for about 1 minute.

5. Add in the cooked vegetables and cook for about 2-3 minutes.

6. Serve hot.

Tofu with Broccoli

Servings: 4

Preparation Time: 20 minutes

Cooking Time: 25 minutes

Ingredients:

For Tofu:

- 14 ounces firm tofu, drained, pressed and cut into 1-inch slices 1/3 cup arrowroot starch, divided
- ¼ cup olive oil
- 1 teaspoon fresh ginger, grated
- 1 medium onion, sliced thinly
- 3 tablespoons low-sodium soy sauce
- 2 tablespoons balsamic vinegar
- 1 tablespoon maple syrup
- ½ cup water

For Steamed Broccoli:

- 2 cups broccoli florets

Directions:

1. In a shallow bowl, place ¼ cup of the arrowroot starch.

2. Add the tofu cubes and coat with arrowroot starch.

3. In a cast-iron wok, heat the olive oil over medium heat and cook the tofu cubes for about 8-10 minutes or until golden from all sides.

4. With a slotted spoon, transfer the tofu cubes onto a plate. Set aside.

5. In the same wok, add ginger and sauté for about 1 minute.

6. Add the onions and sauté for about 2-3 minutes.

7. Add the soy sauce, vinegar and maple syrup and bring to a gentle simmer.

8. In the meantime, in a small bowl, dissolve the remaining arrowroot starch in water.

9. Slowly, add the arrowroot starch mixture into the sauce, stirring continuously.

10. Stir in the cooked tofu and cook for about 1 minute.

11. Meanwhile, in a large pan of water, arrange a steamer basket and bring to a boil.

12. Adjust the heat to medium-low.

13. Place the broccoli florets in the steamer basket and steam, covered for about 5-6 minutes.

14. Remove from the heat and drain the broccoli completely.

15. Transfer the broccoli into the wok of tofu and stir to combine.

16. Serve hot.

Mussel and Potato Stew

Servings: 5

Preparation Time: 10 Minutes.

Cooking Time: 20 Minutes.

Ingredients:

- Potatoes.
- Broccoli.
- Olive oil.
- Filets.
- Garlic.

Directions:

1. Submerge potatoes in cold water in a medium saucepan. Put the salt, and boil. Allow to cook for 15 minutes till soft. Let drain.

2. Boil a saucepan of salted water. Put broccoli rabe, and allow to cook till just soft; it should turn bright green. Drain thoroughly, and slice into 2-inch lengths.

3. In a big, deep skillet, mix garlic, anchovies, and oil. Let cook over high heat for approximately a minute, crushing anchovies. In a skillet, scatter the mussels, put chopped parsley, broccoli rabe, and potatoes on top.

4. Put half cup water, and add salt to season. Place the cover, and allow to cook till mussels are open. Serve.

Broccoli with Bell Peppers

Servings: 6

Preparation Time: 10 minutes

Cooking Time: 10 minutes

Ingredients:

- 2 tablespoons olive oil
- 4 garlic cloves, minced
- 1 large white onion, sliced
- 2 cups small broccoli florets
- 3 red bell peppers, seeded and sliced
- ¼ cup low-sodium vegetable broth
- Salt and ground black pepper, as required

Directions:

1. In a large wok, heat oil over medium heat and sauté the garlic for about 1 minute.

2. Add the onion, broccoli and bell peppers and cook for about 5 minutes, stirring frequently.

3. Stir in the broth and cook for about 4 minutes, stirring frequently.

4. Stir in the salt and black pepper and remove from the heat.

5. Serve hot.

Veggies & Walnut Loaf

Servings: 10

Preparation Time: 15 minutes

Cooking Time: 1 hour 10 minutes

Ingredients:

- 1 tablespoon olive oil
- 2 yellow onions, chopped
- 2 garlic cloves, minced
- 1 teaspoon dried rosemary, crushed
- 1 cup walnuts, chopped
- 2 large carrots, peeled and chopped
- 1 large celery stalk, chopped
- 1 large green bell pepper, seeded and chopped
- 1 cup fresh button mushrooms, chopped
- 5 large eggs
- 1¼ cups almond flour
- Salt and ground black pepper, to taste

Directions:

1. Preheat your oven to 350-degree F.

2. Line 2 loaf pans with lightly greased parchment papers.

3. In a large wok, heat the olive oil over medium heat and sauté the onion for about 4-5 minutes.

4. Add the garlic and rosemary and sauté for about 1 minute.

5. Add the walnuts and vegetables and cook for about 3-4 minutes.

6. Remove the wok from heat and transfer the mixture into a large bowl.

7. Set aside to cool slightly.

8. In another mixing bowl, add the eggs, flour, sea salt, and black pepper, and beat until well combined.

9. Add the egg mixture into the bowl with vegetable mixture and mix until well combined.

10. Divide the mixture into prepared loaf pans evenly.

11. Bake for approximately 50-60 minutes or until top becomes golden-brown.

12. Remove from the oven and set aside to cool slightly.

13. Carefully invert the loaves onto a platter.

14. Cut into desired sized slices and serve.

Shrimp, Spinach & Tomato Casserole

Servings: 6

Preparation Time: 15 minutes

Cooking Time: 25 minutes

Ingredients:

- 2 tablespoon extra-virgin olive oil
- 1 tablespoon garlic, minced
- 1½ pounds large shrimp, peeled and deveined
- ¾ teaspoon dried oregano, crushed
- ½ teaspoon red pepper flakes, crushed
- ¼ cup fresh spinach, chopped finely
- ¾ cup low-sodium chicken broth
- 1 tablespoon fresh lemon juice
- 2 cups tomatoes, chopped
- 4 ounces feta cheese, crumbled

Directions:

1. Preheat your oven to 350 degrees F.

2. In a large skillet, heat the oil over medium-high heat and sauté the garlic for about 1 minute.

3. Add the shrimp, oregano and red pepper flakes and cook for about 4-5 minutes.

4. Stir in the spinach and salt and immediately remove from the heat.

5. Transfer the shrimp mixture into a casserole dish and spread in an even layer.

6. In the same skillet, add the broth and lemon juice over medium heat and simmer for about 3-5 minutes or until reduces to half.

7. Stir in the tomatoes and cook for about 2-3 minutes.

8. Remove from the heat and place the tomato mixture over shrimp mixture evenly.

9. Top with feta cheese evenly.

10. Bake for approximately 15-20 minutes or until top becomes golden brown.

11. Serve hot.

Prawns with Broccoli

Servings: 4

Preparation Time: 20 minutes

Cooking Time: 10 minutes

Ingredients:

- 2 tablespoons olive oil, divided
- 1-pound large prawns, peeled and deveined ½ of onion, chopped
- 3 garlic cloves, minced
- 3 cups broccoli floret
- 2 tablespoons low-sodium soy sauce
- Freshly ground black pepper, as required
- 2 tablespoons fresh parsley, chopped

Directions:

1. In a large non-stick skillet, heat 1 tablespoon of olive oil over medium heat and stir fry the prawns for about 1 minute per side.

2. With a slotted spoon, transfer the prawns onto a plate.

3. In the same skillet, heat the remaining oil over medium heat and sauté the onion and garlic for about 2-3 minutes.

4. Add the broccoli, soy sauce and black pepper and stir fry for about 2-3 minutes.

5. Stir in the cooked prawns and stir fry for about 1-2 minutes.

6. Serve hot.

Prawns with Kale

Servings: 4

Preparation Time: 15 minutes

Cooking Time: 20 minutes

Ingredients:

- 1-pound prawns, peeled and deveined Salt, as required
- 3 tablespoons extra-virgin olive oil, divided
- 1 red onion, chopped finely
- 1 fresh red chili, sliced
- 1-pound fresh kale, tough ribs removed and chopped
- 3 tablespoons low-sodium soy sauce
- 3 tablespoons fresh orange juice
- 1 tablespoon orange zest, grated finely
- ½ teaspoon red pepper flakes, crushed
- Ground black pepper, as required

Directions:

1. Season the prawns with a little salt.

2. In a large non-stick sauté pan, heat 2 tablespoons of olive oil over high heat and stir-fry the prawns for about 2-3 minutes.

3. With a slotted spoon, transfer the prawns onto a plate.

4. In the same sauté pan, heat the remaining oil over medium heat and sauté the onion for about 4-5 minutes.

5. Add the kale and stir-fry for about 2-3 minutes.

6. With a lid, cover the pan and cook for about 2 minutes.

7. Add the soy sauce, orange juice, zest, red pepper flakes and black pepper and stir to combine well.

8. Stir in the cooked prawns and cook for about 2-3 minutes.

9. Serve hot.

Vegetarian Burgers

Servings: 4

Preparation Time: 15 minutes

Cooking Time: 16 minutes

Ingredients:

* 1-pound firm tofu, drained, pressed, and crumbled ¾ cup rolled oats
* ¼ cup flaxseeds
* 2 cups frozen spinach, thawed
* 1 medium onion, chopped finely
* 4 garlic cloves, minced
* 1 teaspoon ground cumin
* 1 teaspoon red pepper flakes, crushed
* Sea salt and freshly ground black pepper, to taste
* 2 tablespoons olive oil
* 6 cups fresh salad greens

Directions:

1. In a large bowl, add all the ingredients except oil and salad greens and mix until well combined.

2. Set aside for about 10 minutes.

3. Make desired size patties from mixture.

4. In a nonstick frying pan, heat the oil over medium heat and cook the patties for 6-8 minutes per side.

5. Serve these patties alongside the salad greens.

Breville Smart Air Fryer Oven Recipes

An air fryer oven is an easy way to cook delicious healthy meals. If you cook your food in oil, it may affect your health but in an air fryer food cooks oil free. An air fryer oven machine uses rapid hot air to circulate around the food. This allows to cook many dishes with meat, vegetables, poultry, fruit, fish and a wide variety of desserts. It is a safer method of cooking and you get the ability to set and leave food to cook most models that have a digital timer. Air fryer cooks can bake, grill, roast and fry providing more options. Although, air fryer toaster oven cooking seems new, professional chefs have been using it for decades in commercial kitchens for its speed and cooking and browning features. Today these ovens are widely available to home cooks at affordable prices.

There are millions of air fryer toaster ovens in private homes today, but people have had to figure out on their own how to adapt their favorite recipes, with varying of success.

Air fryers work by distributing incredibly hot air around the food and don't require oil or fat. You can add a tiny amount to boost taste if you want, however, this generally just a teaspoon full. Which means they are best for anyone and everyone who enjoys yummy healthier food.

They're especially helpful for people who are counting the calories. Dieting may be challenging and usually rules out any fried foods, just from the nature in which they're cooked. Air fryers aren't only for chips! Any sort of food, from chicken bits to pineapple rings could be cooked this manner. The only limiting factor is your own imagination. The air filter removes the need for a nasty skillet at the house. They're practical and simple to wash and make a fantastic addition to any kitchen.

Mixed Veggie Omelet

Servings: 6

Preparation Time: 15 minutes

Cooking Time: 2 hours 13 minutes

Ingredients:

- 1 tablespoon olive oil
- 1 medium onion, chopped
- ¾ cup carrot, peeled and chopped ¾ cup zucchini, chopped
- ¼ cup green bell pepper, seeded and chopped
- ¼ cup red bell pepper, seeded and chopped
- ½ cup low-fat Parmesan cheese, grated
- 8 eggs
- Salt and ground black pepper, as required

Directions:

1. In a skillet, heat the oil over medium heat and cook the onion for about 2-3 minutes.

2. Add the remaining vegetables and cook for about 8-10 minutes.

3. Remove from the heat and set aside to cool slightly.

4. Meanwhile, in a bowl, add cheese, eggs and black pepper and beat until well combined.

5. In a baking dish, place the vegetable mixture.

6. Pour the egg mixture on top evenly.

7. Arrange the baking dish over the wire rack.

8. Select "Slow Cooker" of Breville Smart Air Fryer Oven and set on "High".

9. Set the timer for 2 hours and press "Start/Stop" to begin cooking.

10. When the cooking time is completed, remove the baking dish from the oven and transfer the omelet onto a serving plate.

11. Cut into equal-sized wedges and serve hot.

Bell Pepper Omelet

Servings: 2

Preparation Time: 10 minutes

Cooking Time: 10 minutes

Ingredients:

- 1 teaspoon coconut oil
- 1 small onion, sliced
- ½ of green bell pepper, seeded and chopped
- 4 eggs
- ¼ teaspoon unsweetened almond milk
- Salt and ground black pepper, as required
- ¼ cup low-fat Cheddar cheese, grated

Directions:

1. In a skillet, melt the coconut oil over medium heat and cook the onion and bell pepper for about 4-5 minutes.

2. Remove the skillet from heat and set aside to cool slightly.

3. Meanwhile, in a bowl, add the eggs, milk, salt and black pepper and beat well.

4. Add the cooked onion mixture and gently stir to combine.

5. Place the bell pepper mixture into a small baking dish.

6. Select "Air Fry" of Breville Smart Air Fryer Oven and adjust the temperature to 355 degrees F.

7. Set the timer for 10 minutes and press "Start/Stop" to begin preheating.

8. When the unit beeps to show that it is preheated, arrange the baking dish over the wire rack.

9. When the cooking time is completed, remove the baking dish from oven and place onto a wire rack to cool for about 5 minutes before serving.

10. Cut the omelet into 2 portions and serve hot.

Meaty Breakfast Omelet

Servings: 2

Preparation Time: 10 minutes

Cooking Time 10 minutes

Ingredients:

- 3 large eggs
- 100g ham, cut into small pieces
- ¼ cup milk
- ¾ cup mixed vegetables (mushrooms, scallions, bell pepper) ¼ cup mixed cheddar and mozzarella cheese
- 1 tsp. mixed herbs
- Salt and freshly ground pepper to taste

Directions:

1. Combine the eggs and milk in a medium bowl then add in the remaining ingredients apart from the cheese and mixed herbs and beat well using a fork.

2. Pour the egg mix into an evenly greased pan then place it in the basket of your air fryer toast oven. Cook for roughly 10 minutes at 350°F or until done to desire.

3. Sprinkle the cheese and mixed herbs on the omelet halfway through cook time.

4. Gently loosen the omelet from the sides of the pan using a spatula.

5. Serve hot!

Breakfast Baked Apple

Servings: 2

Preparation Time: 10 minutes

Cooking Time 20 minutes

Ingredients:

- 1 apple
- 2 tbsp. raisins
- 2 tbsp. walnuts, chopped ¼ tsp. nutmeg
- ¼ tsp. ground cinnamon
- 1 ½ tsp. margarine
- ¼ cup water

Directions:

1. Start by setting your air fryer toast oven to 350°F.

2. Cut the apple in half and gently spoon out some of the flesh.

3. Place the apple halves on your air fryer toast ovens frying pan.

4. Mix the raisins, walnuts, nutmeg, cinnamon and margarine in a bowl and divide equally between the apple halves. Pour the water into the pan and cook for 20 minutes.

5. Enjoy!

Citrus Blueberry Muffins

Servings: 3-4

Preparation Time: 15 minutes

Cooking Time 15 minutes

Ingredients:

- 2 ½ cups cake flour
- ½ cup sugar
- ¼ cup light cooking oil such as avocado oil ½ cup heavy cream
- 1 cup fresh blueberries
- 2 eggs
- Zest and juice from 1 orange
- 1 tsp. pure vanilla extract
- 1 tsp. brown sugar for topping

Directions:

1. Start by combining the oil, heavy cream, eggs, orange juice and vanilla extract in a large bowl then set aside. Separately combine the flour and sugar until evenly it's mixed then pour little by little into the wet ingredients. Combine until well blended but be careful not to over-mix.

2. Preheat your air fryer toast oven at 320°F

3. Gently fold the blueberries into the batter and divide into cupcake holders, preferably, silicone cupcake holders as you won't have to grease them. Alternatively, you can use cupcake

paper liners on any cupcake holders/ tray you could be having.

4.   Sprinkle the tops with the brown sugar and pop the muffins in the fryer.

5.   Bake for about 12 minutes. Use a toothpick to check for readiness. When the muffins have evenly browned and an inserted toothpick comes out clean, they are ready.

6.   Take out the muffins and let cool.

7.   Enjoy!

Cheddar Mustard Toasts

Servings: 2

Preparation Time: 10 minutes

Cooking Time: 10 minutes

Ingredients:

*   4 whole-wheat bread slices
*   2 tablespoons low-fat cheddar cheese, shredded
*   2 eggs, whites and yolks, separated
*   1 tablespoon mustard
*   1 tablespoon paprika
*   1 avocado, peeled, pitted and sliced

Directions:

1. In a clean glass bowl, add the egg whites in and beat until they form soft peaks.

2. In another bowl, mix together the cheese, egg yolks, mustard, and paprika.

3. Gently fold in the egg whites.

4. Spread the mustard mixture over the toasted bread slices.

5. Arrange the bread slices in the air fry basket.

6. Select "Air Fry" of Breville Smart Air Fryer Oven and adjust the temperature to 355 degrees F.

7. Set the timer for 10 minutes and press "Start/Stop" to begin preheating.

8. When the unit beeps to show that it is preheated, insert the air fry basket in the oven.

9. When the cooking time is completed, remove the air fry basket from the oven.

10. Serve warm alongside the avocado slices.

Baked Eggs

Servings: 4

Preparation Time: 10 minutes

Cooking Time: 12 minutes

Ingredients:

*   1 cup marinara sauce, divided
*   1 tablespoon capers, drained and divided
*   8 eggs
*   ¼ cup whipping cream, divided
*   ¼ cup low-fat Parmesan cheese, shredded and divided Salt and ground black pepper, as required
*   4 cups fresh baby spinach

Directions:

1. Grease 4 ramekins. Set aside.

2. Divide the marinara sauce in the bottom of each prepared ramekin evenly and top with capers.

3. Carefully crack 2 eggs over marinara sauce into each ramekin and top with cream, followed by the Parmesan cheese.

4. Sprinkle each ramekin with salt and black pepper.

5. Select "Bake" of Breville Smart Air Fryer Oven and adjust the temperature to 400 degrees F.

6. Set the timer for 12 minutes and press "Start/Stop" to begin preheating.

7. When the unit beeps to show that it is preheated, arrange the ramekins over the wire rack.

8. When the cooking time is completed, remove the ramekins from the oven.

9. Serve warm alongside the spinach.

Turkey & Zucchini Omelet

Servings: 6

Preparation Time: 15 minutes

Cooking Time: 35 minutes

Ingredients:

*   8 eggs
*   ½ cup unsweetened almond milk
*   1/8 teaspoon red pepper flakes, crushed
*   Salt and ground black pepper, as required
*   1 cup cooked turkey meat, chopped
*   1 cup low-fat Monterrey Jack cheese, shredded ½ cup fresh scallion, chopped
*   ¾ cup zucchini, chopped

Directions:

1. In a bowl, add the eggs, almond milk, salt and black pepper and beat well.

2. Add the remaining ingredients and stir to combine.

3. Place the mixture into a greased baking dish.

4. Select "Bake" of Breville Smart Air Fryer Oven and adjust the temperature to 315 degrees F.

5. Set the timer for 35 minutes and press "Start/Stop" to begin preheating.

6. When the unit beeps to show that it is preheated, arrange the baking dish over the wire rack.

7. When the cooking time is completed, remove the baking dish from the oven and place onto a wire rack to cool for about 5 minutes before serving.

8. Cut into equal-sized wedges and serve.

Sunny Side up Egg Tarts

Servings: 2

Cooking Time 20 minutes

Ingredients:

- 4 eggs
- ¾ cup shredded Gruyere cheese (or preferred cheese)
- 1 sheet of puff pastry
- Minced chives for topping

Directions:

1. Start by flouring a clean surface then gently roll out your sheet of puff pastry and divide it into four equal squares. If you have a small air fryer toast oven, start with two squares but if it's big enough, go ahead and place the squares on the basket and cook for about 8-10 minutes or until they turn golden brown.

2. Whilst still in the basket, gently make an indentation at the center of each square and sprinkle 2-4 tablespoons of shredded cheese in the well then crack an egg on top.

3. Cook for 5-10 minutes or to desired doneness.

4. Remove from air fryer toast oven, sprinkle with chives and you are ready to eat!

Zucchini Omelet

Servings: 2

Preparation Time: 15 minutes

Cooking Time: 18 minutes

Ingredients:

- 1 teaspoon olive oil
- 1 zucchini, julienned
- 4 eggs

- ¼ teaspoon fresh basil, chopped
- ¼ teaspoon red pepper flakes, crushed
- Salt and ground black pepper, as required

Directions:

1. In a skillet, heat the oil over medium heat and cook the zucchini for about 4-5 minutes.

2. Remove from the heat and set aside to cool slightly.

3. Meanwhile, in a bowl, add the eggs, basil, red pepper flakes, salt and black pepper and beat until well combined.

4. In a baking dish, place the zucchini mixture.

5. Top with egg mixture and gently stir to combine.

6. Select "Air Fry" of Breville Smart Air Fryer Oven and adjust the temperature to 355 degrees F.

7. Set the timer for 10 minutes and press "Start/Stop" to begin preheating.

8. When the unit beeps to show that it is preheated, arrange the baking dish over the wire rack.

9. When the cooking time is completed, remove the baking dish from oven and transfer the omelet onto a plate.

10. Cut into equal-sized wedges and serve hot.

Crunchy Hash Browns

Servings: 3

Preparation Time: 30 minutes

Cooking Time 15 minutes

Ingredients:

- 5 medium potatoes, peeled and grated
- 1 tsp. onion powder
- 1 tsp. garlic powder
- 2 tbsp. corn flour
- 1 ½ tsp. chili flakes
- Salt and freshly ground pepper to taste
- 2 tsp. olive oil

Directions:

1. Put the grated potatoes in a large bowl and cover with ice cold water and let it sit for a minute. Drain the water and repeat this step two times. (This removes the excess starch)

2. Pour 1 teaspoon of oil in a pan, preferably non-stick, over medium heat and sauté the potatoes for about 3 minutes. Transfer the potatoes to a shallow bowl and let cool. Sprinkle

the potatoes with the remaining ingredients and mix until it combines well.

3. Transfer the potato mix to a flat plate and pat it down to make 1 compact layer. Put in the fridge and let it sit for 20 minutes.

4. Set your air fryer toast oven to 360°F.

5. Meanwhile take out the flattened potato and divide into equal portions using a knife or cookie cutter.

6. Lightly brush your air fryer toast oven's basket with the remaining teaspoon of olive oil.

7. Gently place the potato pieces into the greased basket and fry for 12-15 minutes, flipping the hash browns halfway through.

8. Enjoy hot!

Cheese Toasts with Mushrooms

Servings: 2

Preparation Time: 10 minutes

Cooking Time: 4 minutes

Ingredients:

- 4 bread slices
- 1 garlic clove, minced
- 4 ounces goat cheese, crumbled
- Freshly ground black pepper, to taste
- 1 cup cooked mushrooms, sliced
- 2 cups fresh baby spinach

Directions:

1. In a food processor, add the garlic, ricotta, lemon zest and black pepper and pulse until smooth.

2. Spread ricotta mixture over each bread slices evenly.

3. Arrange the bread slices in the air fry basket.

4. Select "Air Fry" of Breville Smart Air Fryer Oven and adjust the temperature to 355 degrees F.

5. Set the timer for 4 minutes and press "Start/Stop" to begin preheating.

6. When the unit beeps to show that it is preheated, insert the air fry basket in the oven.

7. When the cooking time is completed, remove the air fry basket from the oven and transfer the bread slices onto serving plates.

8. Top with mushroom and serve alongside spinach.

Beef & Mushroom Casserole

Servings: 6

Preparation Time: 15 minutes

Cooking Time: 19 minutes

Ingredients:

- 1 tablespoon olive oil
- ½ pound ground beef
- ¾ cup yellow onion, chopped
- 5 fresh mushrooms, sliced
- 8 eggs, beaten
- ½ teaspoon garlic salt
- ¾ cup low-fat Cheddar cheese, shredded and divided ¼ cup sugar-free Alfredo sauce

Directions:

1. In a skillet, heat the oil over medium heat and cook the beef and onions for about 4-5 minutes.

2. Add the mushrooms and cook for about 6-7 minutes.

3. Remove from the oven and drain the grease from the skillet.

4. In a bowl, add the beef mixture, beaten eggs, garlic salt, ½ cup of cheese and Alfredo sauce and stir to combine.

5. Place the beef mixture into a baking dish.

6. Select "Air Fry" of Breville Smart Air Fryer Oven and adjust the temperature to 390 degrees F.

7. Set the timer for 12 minutes and press "Start/Stop" to begin preheating.

8. When the unit beeps to show that it is preheated, arrange the baking dish over the wire rack.

9. After 6 minutes of cooking, stir the sausage mixture well.

10. When the cooking time is completed, remove the baking dish from oven and place onto a wire rack to cool for about 5 minutes before serving.

11. Cut into equal-sized wedges and serve with the topping of remaining cheese.

Beef & Scallion Frittata

Servings: 4

Preparation Time: 15 minutes

Cooking Time: 20 minutes

Ingredients:

- ½ pound cooked ground beef, grease removed

- 1 cup low-fat Colby Jack cheese, shredded
- 8 eggs, beaten lightly
- 4 scallions, chopped
- 1/8 teaspoon red pepper flakes, crushed
- Salt and ground black pepper, as required

Directions:

1. In a bowl, add the beef, cheese, eggs, scallion and cayenne and mix until well combined.

2. Place the mixture into a greased baking dish.

3. Select "Air Fry" of Breville Smart Air Fryer Oven and adjust the temperature to 360 degrees F.

4. Set the timer for 20 minutes and press "Start/Stop" to begin preheating.

5. When the unit beeps to show that it is preheated, arrange the baking dish over the wire rack.

6. When the cooking time is completed, remove the baking dish from oven and place onto a wire rack to cool for about 5 minutes before serving.

7. Cut into 4 wedges and serve.

Chicken & Veggies Frittata

Servings: 8

Preparation Time: 15 minutes Cooking Time: 3 hours

Ingredients:

- 8 eggs
- ½ teaspoon dried parsley
- Pinch of garlic powder
- Salt and ground black pepper, as required
- 1 1/3 cups cooked chicken, chopped finely
- 1½ cups red bell pepper, seeded and chopped
- ¾ cup frozen chopped spinach, thawed and squeezed ¼ cup yellow onion, chopped

Directions:

1. In a bowl, add the eggs, parsley, garlic powder, salt and black pepper and beat well.

2. In a greased baking dish, place the remaining ingredients.

3. Pour the egg mixture over chicken mixture and gently stir to combine.

4. Arrange the baking dish over the wire rack.

5. Select "Slow Cooker" of Breville Smart Air Fryer Oven and set on "Low".

6. Set the timer for 3 hours and press "Start/Stop" to begin cooking.

7. When the cooking time is completed, remove the baking dish from the oven and transfer the frittata onto a serving plate.

8. Cut into 4 equal-sized wedges and serve hot.

Salmon Quiche

Servings: 2

Preparation Time: 15 minutes

Cooking Time: 20 minutes

Ingredients:

- 5½ ounces salmon fillet, chopped
- Salt and ground black pepper, as required ½ tablespoon fresh lemon juice
- 1 egg yolk
- 3½ tablespoons chilled coconut oil 2/3 cups flour
- 1 tablespoon cold water
- 2 eggs
- 3 tablespoons whipping cream
- 1 scallion, chopped

Directions:

1. In a bowl, add the salmon, salt, black pepper and lemon juice and mix well.

2. In another bowl, add the egg yolk, coconut oil, flour and water and mix until a dough forms.

3. Place the dough onto a floured smooth surface and roll into about 7-inch round.

4. Place the dough in a quiche pan and press firmly in the bottom and along the edges.

5. Trim the excess edges.

6. In a small bowl, add the eggs, cream, salt and black pepper and beat until well combined.

7. Place the cream mixture over the crust evenly and top with the salmon mixture, followed by the scallion.

8. Select "Air Fry" of Breville Smart Air Fryer Oven and adjust the temperature to 355 degrees F.

9. Set the timer for 20 minutes and press "Start/Stop" to begin preheating.

10. When the unit beeps to show that it is preheated, arrange the quiche pan over the wire rack.

11. When the cooking time is completed, remove the quiche pan from the oven and set aside for about 5 minutes before serving.

12. Cut the quiche into equal-sized wedges and serve.

Parmesan Eggs in Avocado Cups

Servings: 2

Preparation Time: 10 minutes

Cooking Time: 12 minutes

Ingredients:

- 1 avocado, halved and pitted
- Salt and ground black pepper, as required
- 2 eggs
- 1 tablespoon low-fat Parmesan cheese, shredded

Directions:

1. Arrange a greased square piece of foil in the air fry basket.

2. Select "Bake" of Breville Smart Air Fryer Oven and adjust the temperature to 390 degrees F.

3. Set the timer for 12 minutes and press "Start/Stop" to begin preheating.

4. Meanwhile, carefully scoop out about 2 teaspoons of flesh from each avocado half.

5. Crack 1 egg in each avocado half and sprinkle with salt, black pepper and cheese.

6. When the unit beeps to show that it is preheated, arrange the avocado halves into the prepared air fry basket and insert in the oven.

7. When the cooking time is completed, transfer the avocado halves onto serving plates.

8. Top with Parmesan and serve.

Pasta Salad

Servings: 6

Preparation Time: 10 minutes

Cooking Time: 12 minutes

Ingredients:

- 1 zucchini, sliced in half and roughly chopped
- 1 orange bell pepper, roughly chopped
- 1 green bell pepper, roughly chopped
- 1 red onion, roughly chopped
- 4 ounces' brown mushrooms, halved
- Salt and black pepper to the taste
- 1 tsp. Italian seasoning
- 1-pound penne rig ate, already cooked
- 1 cup cherry tomatoes, halved
- ½ cup Kalamata olive, pitted and halved ¼ cup olive oil
- 3 tbsp. balsamic vinegar
- 2 tbsp. basil, chopped

Directions:

1. In a bowl, mix zucchini with mushrooms, orange bell pepper, green bell pepper, red onion, salt, pepper, Italian seasoning and oil, toss well, transfer to preheated air fryer at 380°F and cook them for 12 minutes.

2. In a large salad bowl, mix pasta with cooked veggies, cherry tomatoes, olives, vinegar and basil, toss and serve for lunch.

Spinach & Tomato Frittata

Servings: 6

Preparation Time: 15 minutes

Cooking Time: 30 minutes

Ingredients:

- 10 large eggs
- Salt and ground black pepper, as required
- 1 (5-ounce) bag baby spinach
- 2 cups grape tomatoes, halved
- 4 scallions, sliced thinly
- 8 ounces feta cheese, crumbled
- 3 tablespoons hot olive oil

Directions:

1. In a bowl, place the eggs, salt and black pepper and beat well.

2. Add the spinach, tomatoes, scallions and feta cheese and gently stir to combine.

3. Spread the oil in a baking dish and top with the spinach mixture.

4. Select "Bake" of Breville Smart Air Fryer Oven and adjust the temperature to 350 degrees F.

5. Set the timer for 30 minutes and press "Start/Stop" to begin preheating.

6. When the unit beeps to show that it is preheated, arrange the baking dish over the wire rack.

7. When the cooking time is completed, remove the baking dish from oven and place onto a wire rack to cool for about 5 minutes before serving.

8. Cut into equal-sized wedges and serve.

Crunchy Zucchini Hash Browns

Servings: 3

Preparation Time: 30 minutes

Cooking Time 15 minutes

Ingredients:

- 4 medium zucchinis, peeled and grated
- 1 tsp. onion powder
- 1 tsp. garlic powder
- 2 tbsp. almond flour
- 1 ½ tsp. chili flakes
- Salt and freshly ground pepper to taste
- 2 tsp. olive oil

Directions:

1. Put the grated zucchini in between layers of kitchen towel and squeeze to drain excess water. Pour 1 teaspoon of oil in a pan, preferably non-stick, over medium heat and sauté the potatoes for about 3 minutes.

2. Transfer the zucchini to a shallow bowl and let cool. Sprinkle it with the remaining ingredients and mix it until it forms a proper mixture.

3. Transfer the zucchini mix to a flat plate and pat it down to make 1 compact layer. Put in the fridge and let it sit for 20 minutes.

4. Set your air fryer toast oven to 360°F.

5. Meanwhile take out the flattened zucchini and divide into equal portions using a knife or cookie cutter.

6. Lightly brush your air fryer toast oven's basket with the remaining teaspoon of olive oil.

7. Gently place the zucchini pieces into the greased basket and fry for 12-15 minutes, flipping the hash browns halfway through.

8. Enjoy hot!

Chicken & Bell Pepper Omelet

Servings: 5
Preparation Time: 15 minutes
Cooking Time: 2¾ minutes

Ingredients:

- ½ cup unsweetened almond milk
- 6 eggs
- 1 garlic clove, minced
- Salt and ground black pepper, as required ¾ cup cooked chicken, chopped
- 1 red bell pepper, seeded and sliced thinly
- 1 small white onion, chopped finely
- 1 cup part-skim mozzarella cheese, shredded

Directions:

1. In a bowl, add the milk, eggs, garlic, salt and black pepper and beat until well combined.

2. In a greased baking dish, place the egg mixture.

3. Add the chicken, bell pepper and onion and stir to combine.

4. Arrange the baking dish over the wire rack.

5. Select "Slow Cooker" of Breville Smart Air Fryer Oven and set on "High".

6. Set the timer for 2¾ hours and press "Start/Stop" to begin cooking.

7. After 2½ hours, sprinkle the omelet with cheese evenly.

8. When the cooking time is completed, remove the baking dish from the oven and transfer the omelet onto a serving plate.

9. Cut into 4 equal-sized wedges and serve hot.

Ham and Cheese sandwich

Servings: 2
Preparation Time: 15 minutes
Cooking Time 20 minutes

Ingredients:

- 2 eggs
- 4 slices of bread of choice
- 4 slices turkey
- 4 slices ham
- 6 tbsp. half and half cream
- 2 tsp. melted butter
- 4 slices Swiss cheese
- ¼ tsp. pure vanilla extract
- Powdered sugar and raspberry jam for serving

Directions:

1. Mix the eggs, vanilla and cream in a bowl and set aside.

2. Make a sandwich with the bread layered with cheese slice, turkey, ham, cheese slice and the top slice of bread to make two sandwiches. Gently press on the sandwiches to somewhat flatten them.

3. Set your air fryer toast oven to 350°F.

4. Spread out kitchen aluminum foil and cut it about the same size as the sandwich and spread the melted butter on the surface of the foil.

5. Dip the sandwich in the egg mixture and let it soak for about 20 seconds on each side. Repeat this for the other sandwich. Place the soaked sandwiches on the prepared foil sheets then place on the basket in your fryer.

6. Cook for 12 minutes then flip the sandwiches and brush with the remaining butter and cook for another 5 minutes or until well browned.

7. Place the cooked sandwiched on a plate and top with the powdered sugar and serve with a small bowl of raspberry jam.

8. Enjoy!

Eggs with Turkey

Servings: 2

Preparation Time: 10 minutes

Cooking Time: 13 minutes

Ingredients:

- 2 teaspoons coconut oil, softened
- 2 ounces cooked turkey breast, sliced thinly
- 4 large eggs, divided
- 1 tablespoon coconut milk
- Salt and ground black pepper, as required 1/8 teaspoon smoked paprika
- 3 tablespoons low-fat Parmesan cheese, grated finely
- 2 teaspoons fresh chives, minced

Directions:

1. In the bottom of a baking dish, spread the coconut oil.

2. Arrange the turkey slices over the coconut oil.

3. In a bowl, add 1egg, coconut milk, salt and black pepper and beat until smooth.

4. Place the egg mixture over the turkey slices evenly.

5. Carefully crack the remaining eggs on top and sprinkle with paprika, salt, black pepper, cheese and chives evenly.

6. Select "Air Fry" of Breville Smart Air Fryer Oven and adjust the temperature to 320 degrees F.

7. Set the timer for 13 minutes and press "Start/Stop" to begin preheating.

8. When the unit beeps to show that it is preheated, arrange the baking dish over the wire rack.

9. When the cooking time is completed, remove the baking dish from the oven and set aside for about 5 minutes before serving.

10. Cut into equal-sized wedges and serve.

Eggs with Turkey & Spinach

Servings: 4

Preparation Time: 15 minutes

Cooking Time: 23 minutes

Ingredients:

- 1 tablespoon coconut oil
- 1-pound fresh baby spinach
- 4 eggs
- 7 ounces cooked turkey, chopped
- 4 teaspoons unsweetened almond milk
- Salt and ground black pepper, as required

Directions:

1. In a skillet, melt the coconut oil over medium heat and cook the spinach for about 2-3 minutes or until just wilted.

2. Remove from the heat and transfer the spinach into a bowl.

3. Set aside to cool slightly.

4. Divide the spinach into 4 greased ramekins, followed by the turkey.

5. Crack 1 egg into each ramekin and drizzle with almond milk.

6. Sprinkle with salt and black pepper.

7. Select "Air Fry" of Breville Smart Air Fryer Oven and adjust the temperature to 355 degrees F.

8. Set the timer for 20 minutes and press "Start/Stop" to begin preheating.

9. When the unit beeps to show that it is preheated, arrange the ramekins over the wire rack.

10. When the cooking time is completed, remove the ramekins from oven and place onto a wire rack to cool for about 5 minutes before serving.

Mini Veggie Frittatas

Servings: 2

Preparation Time: 15 minutes

Cooking Time: 17 minutes

Ingredients:

- 1 tablespoon coconut oil
- ½ of white onion, sliced thinly
- 1 cup fresh mushrooms, sliced thinly
- 1¼ cups fresh spinach, chopped
- 3 eggs
- ½ teaspoon fresh rosemary, chopped

- Salt and ground black pepper, as required
- 3 tablespoons low-fat Parmesan cheese, shredded

Directions:

1. In a frying pan, melt coconut oil over medium heat and cook the onion and mushroom for about 3 minutes.

2. Add the spinach and cook for about 2-3 minutes.

3. Remove the frying pan from heat and set aside to cool slightly.

4. Meanwhile, in a small bowl, add the eggs, rosemary, salt and black pepper and beat well.

5. Divide the beaten eggs in 2 greased ramekins evenly and top with the veggie mixture, followed by the cheese.

6. Select "Air Fry" of Breville Smart Air Fryer Oven and adjust the temperature to 330 degrees F.

7. Set the timer for 12 minutes and press "Start/Stop" to begin preheating.

8. When the unit beeps to show that it is preheated, place the ramekins over the air rack.

9. When the cooking time is completed, remove the ramekins from oven and place onto a wire rack for about 5 minutes before serving.

Fish and Chips

Servings: 2

Preparation Time: 10 minutes

Cooking Time: 12 minutes

Ingredients:

- 2 medium cod fillets, skinless and boneless Salt and black pepper to the taste
- ¼ cup margarine milk
- 3 cups kettle chips, cooked

Directions:

1. In a bowl, mix fish with salt, pepper and margarine milk, toss and leave aside for 5 minutes. Put chips in your food processor, crush them and spread them on a plate.

2. Add fish and press well on all sides.

3. Transfer fish to your air fryer's basket and cook at 400 °F for 12 minutes. Serve hot for lunch.

Chicken Casserole

Servings: 6

Preparation Time: 10 Minutes

Cooking Time: 9 minutes

Ingredients:

- 3 cup chicken, shredded
- 12 oz. bag egg noodles
- 1/2 large onion
- 1/2 cup chopped carrots
- 1/4 cup frozen peas
- 1/4 cup frozen broccoli pieces
- 2 stalks celery chopped
- 5 cup chicken broth
- 1 teaspoon garlic powder
- Salt and pepper to taste
- 1 cup cheddar cheese, shredded
- 1 package French's onions 1/4 c sour cream
- 1 can cream of chicken and mushroom soup

Directions:

1. Add chicken, broth, black pepper, salt, garlic powder, vegetables, and egg noodles to the Instant Pot Duo. Put on the pressure-cooking lid and seal it.

2. Hit the "Pressure Button" and select 4 minutes of cooking time, then press "Start." Once the Instant Pot Duo beeps, do a quick release and remove its lid.

3. Stir in cheese, 1/3 of French's onions, can of soup and sour cream.

4. Mix well and spread the remaining onion top.

5. Put on the Air Fryer lid and seal it.

6. Hit the "Air fryer Button" and select 5 minutes of cooking time, then press "Start." Once the Instant Pot Duo beeps, remove its lid.

7. Serve.

Cranberry Muffins

Servings: 8

Preparation Time: 25 minutes

Cooking Time: 15 minutes

Ingredients:

- ¼ cup unsweetened almond milk
- 2 large eggs
- ½ teaspoon vanilla extract 1½ cups almond flour ¼ cup Erythritol
- 1 teaspoon baking powder

- ¼ teaspoon ground cinnamon 1/8 teaspoon salt
- ½ cup fresh cranberries
- ¼ cup walnuts, chopped

Directions:

1. In a blender, add the almond milk, eggs and vanilla extract and pulse for about 20-30 seconds.

2. Add the almond flour, Erythritol, baking powder, cinnamon and salt and pulse for about 30-45 seconds until well blended.

3. Transfer the mixture into a bowl.

4. Gently fold in half of the cranberries and walnuts.

5. Place the mixture into 8 silicone muffin cups and top each with remaining cranberries.

6. Select "Air Fry" of Breville Smart Air Fryer Oven and adjust the temperature to 325 degrees F.

7. Set the timer for 15 minutes and press "Start/Stop" to begin preheating.

8. When the unit beeps to show that it is preheated, arrange the muffin cups over the wire rack.

9. When the cooking time is completed, remove the muffin cups from oven and place onto a wire rack to cool for about 10 minutes.

10. Carefully invert the muffins onto the wire rack to completely cool before serving.

Garlicky Fish Fingers

Servings: 4
Preparation Time: 10 minutes
Cooking Time: 10 minutes

Ingredients:

- 2/3 lb. white fish, boneless, cut into fingers
- ½ tsp. salt
- 2 tbsp. lemon juice
- ½ tsp. turmeric powder
- ½ tsp. red chili flakes
- 2 tsp. mixed dried herbs, divided
- 2 tsp. garlic powder, divided
- ½ tsp. crushed black pepper
- 1 tsp. ginger garlic paste
- 2 tbsp. flour
- 1 tsp. rice flour
- 2 tsp. corn flour
- 2 egg
- ¼ tsp. baking soda
- 1 cup breadcrumbs
- Oil for brushing

Directions:

1. Beat eggs with lemon juice and garlic paste in a shallow bowl, mix corn flour with rice flour, black pepper, garlic powder, herbs, chili flakes, turmeric powder, salt, and baking soda in another tray.

2. Coat the fish fingers with flour mixture, then dip in the egg and coat with the breadcrumbs. Place the fish fingers in the Air Fryer basket.

3. Spray the fingers with cooking oil. Set the basket inside the Air Fryer toaster oven and close the lid.

4. Air Fry at 356°F temperature for 10 minutes. Serve warm.

Chicken & Cauliflower Casserole

Servings: 5
Preparation Time: 15 minutes
Cooking Time: 35 minutes

Ingredients:

- 1½ tablespoons olive oil
- ½ of large onion, chopped
- 24 ounces cauliflower rice
- 3 eggs
- 2 tablespoons unsweetened almond milk
- Salt and ground black pepper, as required
- ½ pound cooked chicken, chopped
- ¼ cup low-fat Cheddar cheese, shredded

Directions:

1. In a skillet, heat the oil over medium heat and sauté the onion for about 4-5 minutes.

2. Remove from the heat and transfer the onion into a bowl.

3. Add the cauliflower rice and mix well.

4. Place the mixture into a baking dish.

5. Select "Bake" of Breville Smart Air Fryer Oven and adjust the temperature to 350 degrees F.

6. Set the timer for 32 minutes and press "Start/Stop" to begin preheating.

7. When the unit beeps to show that it is preheated, arrange the baking dish over the wire rack.

8. Stir the mixture once after 8 minutes.

9. Meanwhile, in a bowl, add the eggs, milk, salt and black pepper and beat well.

10. After 15 minutes of cooking, place the egg mixture over cauliflower rice mixture evenly and top with the chicken pieces.

11. After 30 minutes of cooking, sprinkle the casserole with the cheese.

12. When the cooking time is completed, remove the baking dish from oven and

place onto a wire rack to cool for about 5 minutes before serving.

13. Cut into equal-sized wedges and serve.

Healthy Spinach Scramble

Servings: 1

Preparation Time: 8 minutes

Cooking Time 30 minutes

Ingredients:

* 3 egg whites
* 1 cup (packed) spinach
* 1 onion, chopped
* 2 tbsp. extra virgin olive oil ½ tsp. onion powder
* ½ tsp. garlic powder
* 1 tsp. turmeric powder
* Ground pepper to taste

Directions:

1. Preheat your air fryer toast oven to 350°F.

2. Beat the egg whites and oil in a large bowl. Add in the fresh ingredients and mix until well combined then set the bowl aside.

3. Lightly grease your air fryer toast oven's frying pan and transfer the egg mixture into the pan. Cook in the fryer for about 10 minutes or until done to desire.

4. Serve hot.

Mixed Veggies Soup

Servings: 6

Preparation Time: 15 minutes

Cooking Time: 8 hours 5 minutes

Ingredients:

* 1 tablespoon olive oil
* 1 yellow onion, chopped
* 1 celery stalk, chopped
* 1 large carrot, peeled and chopped
* 2 garlic cloves, minced
* 1 teaspoon dried oregano, crushed

* 1 large zucchini, chopped
* 2 tomatoes, chopped
* 1 cup fresh spinach, chopped
* 4 cups homemade low-sodium vegetable broth
* Salt and ground black pepper, as required

Directions:

1. In an oven-safe pan that will fit in the Breville Smart Air Fryer Oven, heat the oil over medium heat and sauté the onion, celery and carrot for about 3-4 minutes.

2. Add the garlic and thyme and sauté for about 1 minute.

3. Remove from the heat and stir in the remaining ingredients.

4. Cover the pan with a lid.

5. Arrange the pan over the wire rack.

6. Select "Slow Cooker" of Breville Smart Air Fryer Oven and set on "Low".

7. Set the timer for 8 hours and press "Start/Stop" to begin cooking.

8. When the cooking time is completed, remove the pan from the oven.

9. Remove the lid and stir the mixture well.

10. Serve hot.

Braised Pork

Servings: 2

Preparation Time: 40 minutes

Cooking Time: 40 minutes

Ingredients:

* 1-pound pork loin roast, boneless and cubed
* 2 tablespoons butter, melted and divided Salt and black pepper, to taste
* 1 cup chicken stock
* ¼ cup dry white wine
* 1 clove garlic, minced
* ½ teaspoon thyme, chopped ½ thyme sprig
* 1 bay leaf
* ¼ yellow onion, chopped
* 1 tablespoon white flour
* ¼ pound red grapes

Directions:

1. Season pork cubes with salt and pepper. Rub with half the melted butter and put in the air fryer. Cook at 370F for 8 minutes.

2.   Meanwhile, heat a pan on the stove with 2 tablespoons of butter over medium heat. Add onion and garlic, and stir-fry for 2 minutes.

3.   Add bay leaf, flour, thyme, salt, pepper, stock, and wine. Mix well. Bring to a simmer and take off the heat. Add grapes and pork cubes. Cook in the air fryer at 360°F for 30 minutes.

4.   Serve.

Onion Soup

Servings: 6

Preparation Time: 15 minutes

Cooking Time: 5 hours 10 minutes

Ingredients:

- 2 tablespoons olive oil
- 2 medium sweet onions, sliced
- 2 garlic cloves, minced
- ¼ cup low-sodium soy sauce
- 1 teaspoon unsweetened applesauce
- 1 teaspoon dried oregano, crushed
- 1 teaspoon dried basil, crushed
- Ground black pepper, as required
- 5 cups low-sodium vegetable broth
- ¼ cup low-fat Parmesan cheese, grated

Directions:

1. In an oven-safe pan that will fit in the Breville Smart Air Fryer Oven, heat the oil over medium heat and cook the onion for about 8-9 minutes.

2. Add the garlic and cook for about 1 minute.

3. Remove from the heat and stir in the remaining ingredients except for cheese.

4. Cover the pan with a lid.

5. Arrange the pan over the wire rack.

6. Select "Slow Cooker" of Breville Smart Air Fryer Oven and set on "Low".

7. Set the timer for 5 hours and press "Start/Stop" to begin cooking.

8. When the cooking time is completed, remove the pan from the oven.

9. Remove the lid and stir in the cheese until melted completely.

10.Serve hot.

Beef & Spinach Stew

Servings: 10

Preparation Time: 15 minutes

Cooking Time: 6 hours 10 minutes

Ingredients:

- ¼ cup olive oil, divided
- 2½ pounds beef stew meat, cubed
- Salt and ground black pepper, as required
- 2 small onions, chopped
- 1 teaspoon dried thyme, crushed
- 1 teaspoon dried oregano, crushed
- 1 teaspoon dried basil, crushed
- 1 cup carrot, peeled and chopped
- 1 celery stalk, chopped
- 10 cups fresh spinach, chopped
- 1 cup fresh tomatoes, chopped finely
- 2 cups chicken broth
- 3 tablespoons fresh lemon juice

Directions:

1. In an oven-safe pan that will fit in the Breville Smart Air Fryer Oven, heat 2 tablespoons of the oil over medium heat and cook the beef cubes with salt and black pepper for about 4-5 minutes.

2. With a slotted spoon, transfer the beef cubes into a bowl.

3. In the pan, add the remaining oil and onions and cook for about 4-5 minutes.

4. Remove from the heat and stir in the cooked beef and remaining ingredients except for lemon juice.

5. Cover the pan with a lid.

6. Arrange the pan over the wire rack.

7. Select "Slow Cooker" of Breville Smart Air Fryer Oven and set on "Low".

8. Set the timer for 6 hours and press "Start/Stop" to begin cooking.

9. When the cooking time is completed, remove the pan from the oven and serve hot.

10.Open the lid and stir in the lemon juice.

11.Serve hot.

Peach-Bourbon Wings

Servings: 8

Preparation Time: 5 minutes

Cooking Time: 14 minutes

Ingredients:

- ½ cup peach preserves
- 1 tbsp. brown sugar
- 1 garlic clove, minced
- ¼ tsp. salt

- 2 tbsp. white vinegar
- 2 tbsp. bourbon
- 1 tsp. cornstarch
- 1½ tsp. water
- 2 lbs. chicken wings

Directions:

1. Let your air fryer preheat at 400°F.

2. Add salt, garlic, and brown sugar to a food processor and blend well until smooth. Transfer this mixture to a saucepan and add bourbon, peach preserves, and vinegar. Stir cook this mixture to a boil then reduce heat to a simmer.

3. Cook for 6 minutes until the mixture thickens.

4. Mix cornstarch with water and pour this mixture in the saucepan.

5. Stir cook for 2 minutes until it thickens. Keep ¼ cup of this sauce aside.

6. Place the wings in the air fryer basket and brush them with prepared sauce.

7. Return the fryer basket to the air fryer and cook on air fry mode for 6 minutes at 350°F. Flip the wings and brush them again with the sauce.

8. Air fry the wings for another 8 minutes. Serve with reserved sauce.

Savory Carrot Muffins

Servings: 6

Preparation Time: 15 minutes

Cooking Time: 7 minutes

Ingredients:

For Muffins:

- ¼ cup whole-wheat flour
- ¼ cup all-purpose flour
- ½ teaspoon baking powder
- 1/8 teaspoon baking soda
- ½ teaspoon dried parsley, crushed ½ teaspoon salt
- ½ cup low-fat plain yogurt
- 1 teaspoon vinegar
- 1 tablespoon olive oil
- 3 tablespoons cottage cheese, grated
- 1 carrot, peeled and grated
- 2-4 tablespoons water (if needed)

For Topping:

- 7 ounces low-fat Parmesan cheese, grated ¼ cup walnuts, chopped

Directions:

1. For muffins: in a large bowl, mix together the flours, baking powder, baking soda, parsley, and salt.

2. In another large bowl, add the yogurt and vinegar and mix well.

3. Add the remaining ingredients except for water and beat them well. (Add some water if needed).

4. Make a well in the center of the yogurt mixture.

5. Slowly add the flour mixture in the well and mix until well combined.

6. Place the mixture into lightly greased 6 medium-sized muffin molds evenly and top with the Parmesan cheese and walnuts.

7. Select "Air Fry" of Breville Smart Air Fryer Oven and adjust the temperature to 355 degrees F.

8. Set the timer for 7 minutes and press "Start/Stop" to begin preheating.

9. When the unit beeps to show that it is preheated, arrange the muffin molds over the wire rack.

10. When the cooking time is completed, remove the muffin molds from the oven and place onto a wire rack to cool for about 5 minutes.

11. Carefully invert the muffins onto the platter and serve warm.

Chicken & Spinach Soup

Servings: 6

Preparation Time: 15 minutes

Cooking Time: 6 hours

Ingredients:

- 2 tablespoons coconut oil, melted
- 4 cups cooked chicken, chopped
- 8 cups fresh spinach, chopped
- 1 large carrot, peeled and chopped
- 1 small onion, chopped finely
- ½ tablespoon garlic, minced
- Salt and ground black pepper, as required
- 6 cups low-sodium chicken broth

Directions:

1. In an oven-safe pan that will fit in the Breville Smart Air Fryer Oven, place all ingredients and stir to combine.

2. Cover the pan with a lid.

3. Arrange the pan over the wire rack.

4. Select "Slow Cooker" of Breville Smart Air Fryer Oven and set on "Low".

5. Set the timer for 6 hours and press "Start/Stop" to begin cooking.

6. When the cooking time is completed, remove the pan from the oven.

7. Remove the lid and serve hot.

Lamb Shanks

Servings: 2

Preparation Time: 10 minutes

Cooking Time: 45 minutes

Ingredients:

- 2 lamb shanks
- ½ yellow onion, chopped
- ½ tablespoon olive oil
- 2 teaspoons crushed coriander seeds
- 1 tablespoon white flour
- 2 bay leaves
- 1 teaspoon honey
- 2 ½ ounces dry sherry
- 1 ¼ cups chicken stock
- Salt and pepper, to taste

Directions:

1. Season the lamb shanks with salt and pepper. Rub with half of the oil and cook in the air fryer at 360F for 10 minutes.

2. Heat up a pan with the rest of the oil over medium-high heat. Add onion and coriander. Stir and cook for 5 minutes.

3. Add salt, pepper, bay leaves, honey, stock, sherry, and flour. Bring to a simmer while stirring, then add the lamb.

4. Mix well.

5. Cook in the air fryer at 360°F for 30 minutes.

6. Serve.

Ranch Chicken Wings

Servings: 6

Preparation Time: 10 minutes

Cooking Time: 35 minutes

Ingredients:

- 12 chicken wings
- 1 tablespoon olive oil
- 1 cup chicken broth
- 1/4 cup butter
- 1/2 cup Red Hot Sauce
- 1/4 teaspoon Worcestershire sauce
- 1 tablespoon white vinegar
- 1/4 teaspoon cayenne pepper
- 1/8 teaspoon garlic powder
- Seasoned salt to taste
- Ranch dressing for dipping Celery for garnish

Directions:

1. Set the Air Fryer Basket in the Instant Pot Duo and pour the broth in it.

2. Spread the chicken wings in the basket and put on the pressure-cooking lid.

3. Hit the "Pressure Button" and select 10 minutes of cooking time, then press "Start."

4. Meanwhile, prepare the sauce and add butter, vinegar, cayenne pepper, garlic powder, Worcestershire sauce, and hot sauce in a small saucepan.

5. Stir cook this sauce for 5 minutes on medium heat until it thickens.

6. Once the Instant Pot Duo beeps, do a quick release and remove its lid. Remove the wings and empty the Instant Pot Duo.

7. Toss the wings with oil, salt, and black pepper.

8. Set the Air Fryer Basket in the Instant Pot Duo and arrange the wings in it. Put on the Air Fryer lid and seal it.

9. Hit the "Air Fryer Button" and select 20 minutes of cooking time, then press "Start." Once the Instant Pot beeps, remove its lid.

10. Transfer the wings to the sauce and mix well.

11. Serve.

Chicken & Carrot Stew

Servings: 6

Preparation Time: 15 minutes

Cooking Time: 6 hours

Ingredients:

- 4 (5-ounce) boneless chicken breast, cubed
- 3 cups carrots, peeled and cubed
- 2 celery stalks, chopped
- 1 medium yellow onion, chopped
- 2 garlic cloves, minced

- Salt and ground black pepper, as required ½ teaspoon dried thyme
- ½ teaspoon dried rosemary
- 2 cups chicken broth
- 2 tablespoons olive oil

Directions:

1. In an oven-safe pan that will fit in the Breville Smart Air Fryer Oven, place all ingredients except for oil and stir to combine.

2. Cover the pan with a lid.

3. Arrange the pan over the wire rack.

4. Select "Slow Cooker" of Breville Smart Air Fryer Oven and set on "Low".

5. Set the timer for 6 hours and press "Start/Stop" to begin cooking.

6. When the cooking time is completed, remove the pan from the oven and serve hot.

7. Open the lid and stir in the oil.

8. Serve hot.

Beef and Cheese Enchiladas

Servings: 4

Preparation Time: 10 minutes

Cooking Time: 20 minutes

Ingredients:

- 1 Lb. ground beef
- 1 Tablespoon taco seasoning
- 8 Gluten free tortillas
- 1 Can black beans (rinsed)
- 1 Can diced tomatoes
- 1 Can chopped green chilies
- 1 Cup Mexican cheese (shredded)
- 1 Can red Enchilada sauce
- 1 Cup fresh cilantro (chopped) ½ Cup sour Cream

Directions:

1. The ground beef should be cooked in a frying pan till brown. The cooked beef should be covered by taco seasonings.

2. The tomatoes, beans, chilies should be added to the beef and mixed thoroughly. The mixture is used to cover the tortillas followed by enchiladas sauce.

3. The air fryer should be preheated at 355°F for 5 min. The tortillas are placed in the basket and topping is done by cheese. They are heated for 6 min with intermittent flipping.

4. The cooked tortillas are removed from the basket, topped with cilantro and cream and served hot.

Asian Style Vegetable with Beef

Servings: 4

Preparation Time: 10 minutes

Cooking Time: 10 minutes

Ingredients:

- 1 lb. sirloin steak
- 2 Tablespoons corn starch
- 1 Red pepper (sliced)
- ½ Yellow onion (sliced)
- 1 Tablespoon garlic (minced)
- 2 Tablespoons ginger (grated) 1/2 Cup soy sauce
- 1 Tablespoon sesame oil
- 1/4 Cup rice vinegar
- 1/3 Cup brown sugar
- 1/4 Cup water

Directions:

1. The steak should be cut into strips. All the ingredients are mixed thoroughly to form a mixture to marinade.

2. The steak strips are placed inside a zip bag to which is added the mixture is added and kept in the refrigerator overnight to marinade.

3. The steak pieces are removed from the bag by tongs and placed in the cutting board for 5 min.

4. The air fryer toaster oven should be preheated at 390 F for 5 min. The basket should be covered by aluminum foil.

5. The steaks are placed in the basket and heated for 6 min with intermittent flipping.

6. The cooked steaks are removed from the basket, garnished with scallions and sesame seeds and served hot.

Beef & Mushroom Stew

Servings: 8

Preparation Time: 15 minutes

Cooking Time: 8 hours

Ingredients:

- 2 pounds beef stew meat, cubed
- 2 cups fresh mushrooms, sliced
- 4 garlic cloves, minced

- 1 cup fresh parsley leaves, chopped
- 2 cups tomato paste
- 2 cups beef broth
- Salt and ground black pepper, as required

Directions:

1. In an oven-safe pan that will fit in the Breville Smart Air Fryer Oven, place all ingredients and stir to combine.

2. Cover the pan with a lid.

3. Arrange the pan over the wire rack.

4. Select "Slow Cooker" of Breville Smart Air Fryer Oven and set on "Low".

5. Set the timer for 8 hours and press "Start/Stop" to begin cooking.

6. When the cooking time is completed, remove the pan from the oven and serve hot.

7. Open the lid and serve hot.

Salmon & Veggie Stew

Servings: 4

Preparation Time: 15 minutes

Cooking Time: 6 hours

Ingredients:

- 1-pound salmon fillet, cubed
- 1 tablespoon coconut oil
- 1 medium yellow onion, chopped
- 1 garlic clove, minced
- 1 zucchini, sliced
- 1 green bell pepper, seeded and cubed ½ cup tomatoes, chopped
- ½ cup fish broth
- ¼ teaspoon dried oregano
- ¼ teaspoon dried basil
- Salt and ground black pepper, as required

Directions:

1. In an oven-safe pan that will fit in the Breville Smart Air Fryer Oven, place all ingredients and stir to combine.

2. Cover the pan with a lid.

3. Arrange the pan over the wire rack.

4. Select "Slow Cooker" of Breville Smart Air Fryer Oven and set on "Low".

5. Set the timer for 5-6 hours and press "Start/Stop" to begin cooking.

6. When the cooking time is completed, remove the pan from the oven and serve hot.

Thyme Turkey Tenderloins

Servings: 4

Preparation Time: 10 minutes

Cooking Time: 20 minutes

Ingredients:

- 1 teaspoon dried thyme, crushed
- 1 teaspoon garlic powder
- Salt and ground black pepper, as required
- 1 (24-ounce) package boneless turkey breast tenderloins
- 2 tablespoon olive oil
- 6 cups fresh salad greens

Directions:

1. In a small bowl, mix together the thyme, garlic powder, salt and black pepper.

2. Rub the turkey tenderloin with thyme mixture evenly.

3. In a large skillet, heat the oil over medium heat and cook the turkey tenderloins for about 10 minutes or until golden brown.

4. Remove from the heat.

5. Place the turkey tenderloins over the wire rack.

6. Select "Bake" of Breville Smart Air Fryer Oven and adjust the temperature to 350 degrees F.

7. Set the timer for 10 minutes and press "Start/Stop" to begin preheating.

8. When the unit beeps to show that it is preheated, insert the wire rack in the oven.

9. When the cooking time is completed, remove the wire rack from the oven and serve hot alongside the salad greens.

Crumbly Beef Meatballs

Servings: 6

Preparation Time: 8 minutes

Cooking Time 20 minutes

Ingredients:

- 2 lbs. of ground beef
- 2 large eggs
- 1-1/4 cup panko breadcrumbs
- 1/4 cup chopped fresh parsley
- 1 tsp. dried oregano
- 1/4 cup grated Parmigianino Reggiano
- 1 small clove garlic chopped
- salt and pepper to taste

- 1 tsp. vegetable oil

Directions:

1. Thoroughly mix beef with eggs, crumbs, parsley, and rest of the ingredients.

2. Make small meatballs out of this mixture and place them in the Air Fryer basket.

3. Set the basket inside the Air Fryer toaster oven and close the lid.

4. Select the Air Fry mode at 350°F temperature for 13 minutes.

5. Toss the meatballs after 5 minutes and resume cooking. Serve fresh.

Pork & Cabbage Stew

Servings: 8

Preparation Time: 15 minutes

Cooking Time: 7½ hours

Ingredients:

- 2½ pounds boneless pork meat, cubed into 2-inch size 2½ cups cabbage, chopped
- 2 cups tomatoes, chopped finely
- 1 medium onion, chopped
- 2 garlic cloves, minced
- 2 tablespoon olive oil
- 4 cups chicken broth
- 1 tablespoon fresh oregano, minced
- Salt and ground black pepper, as required
- 3 tablespoon fresh lime juice

Directions:

1. In an oven-safe pan that will fit in the Breville Smart Air Fryer Oven, place all ingredients and stir to combine.

2. Cover the pan with a lid.

3. Arrange the pan over the wire rack.

4. Select "Slow Cooker" of Breville Smart Air Fryer Oven and set on "Low".

5. Set the timer for 7½ hours and press "Start/Stop" to begin cooking.

6. When the cooking time is completed, remove the pan from the oven and serve hot.

7. Open the lid and transfer pork into a large bowl.

8. With 2 forks, shred the meat.

9. Return the shredded pork into the pan and mix well.

10. Serve hot with the drizzling of lime juice.

Seasoned Cauliflower Chunks

Servings: 4

Preparation Time: 10 minutes

Cooking Time 15 minutes

Ingredients:

- 1 cauliflower head, diced into chunks ½ cup unsweetened milk
- 6 tbsp. mayo
- ¼ cup all-purpose flour
- ¾ cup almond meal
- ¼ cup almond meal
- 1 tsp. onion powder
- 1 tsp. garlic powder
- 1 tsp. of sea salt
- ½ tsp. paprika
- Pinch of black pepper
- Cooking oil spray

Directions:

1. Toss cauliflower with rest of the ingredients in a bowl then transfers to the Air Fryer basket.

2. Spray them with cooking oil.

3. Set the basket inside the Air Fryer toaster oven and close the lid.

4. Select the Air Fry mode at 400°F temperature for 15 minutes.

5. Toss well and serve warm.

Marinated Chicken Legs

Servings: 4

Preparation Time: 15 minutes

Cooking Time: 20 minutes

Ingredients:

- 4 chicken legs
- 3 tablespoons fresh lemon juice
- 3 teaspoons ginger paste
- 3 teaspoons garlic paste Salt, as required
- 4 tablespoons low-fat plain yogurt
- 2 teaspoons red chili powder
- 1 teaspoon ground cumin
- 1 teaspoon ground coriander
- 1 teaspoon ground turmeric
- Ground black pepper, as required
- 6 cups fresh baby kale

Directions:

1. In a bowl, chicken legs, lemon juice, ginger paste, garlic paste, and salt and mix well.

2. Set aside for about 15 minutes.

3. Meanwhile, in another bowl, mix together the yogurt, spices, and food color.

4. Add the chicken legs into bowl and generously coat with the spice mixture.

5. Cover the bowl of chicken and refrigerate for at least 10-12 hours.

6. Arrange the chicken legs into the greased air fry basket.

7. Select "Air Fry" of Breville Smart Air Fryer Oven and adjust the temperature to 445 degrees F.

8. Set the timer for 20 minutes and press "Start/Stop" to begin preheating.

9. When the unit beeps to show that it is preheated, insert the air fry basket in the oven.

10. When the cooking time is completed, remove the air fry basket from the oven and serve hot alongside the kale.

Seafood & Spinach Stew

Servings: 8

Preparation Time: 20 minutes

Cooking Time: 4 hours 50 minutes

Ingredients:

- 2 tablespoons olive oil
- ½ pound tomatoes, chopped
- 1 large yellow onion, chopped finely
- 2 garlic cloves, minced
- 2 teaspoons curry powder
- 6 sprigs fresh parsley
- Salt and ground black pepper, as required 1½ cups chicken broth
- 1½ pounds salmon, cut into cubes
- 1½ pounds shrimp, peeled and deveined 1-pound fresh spinach, chopped

Directions:

1. In an oven-safe pan that will fit in the Breville Smart Air Fryer Oven, place all ingredients except for seafood and spinach and stir to combine.

2. Cover the pan with a lid.

3. Arrange the pan over the wire rack.

4. Select "Slow Cooker" of Breville Smart Air Fryer Oven and set on "Low".

5. Set the timer for 4 hours and press "Start/Stop" to begin cooking.

6. When the cooking time is completed, remove the pan from the oven.

7. Open the lid and stir in the seafood and spinach.

8. Cover the pan with a lid.

9. Arrange the pan over the wire rack.

10. Select "Slow Cooker" of Breville Smart Air Fryer Oven and set on "Low".

11. Set the timer for 50 minutes and press "Start/Stop" to begin cooking.

12. When the cooking time is completed, remove the pan from the oven and serve hot.

Sweet & Spicy Chicken Drumsticks

Servings: 4

Preparation Time: 15 minutes

Cooking Time: 20 minutes

Ingredients:

- 1 garlic clove, crushed
- 1 teaspoon cayenne pepper
- 1 teaspoon red chili powder
- 2 teaspoons Erythritol
- 1 tablespoon mustard
- Salt and ground black pepper, as required
- 1 tablespoon olive oil
- 4 (6-ounce) chicken drumsticks
- 6 cups lettuce, torn

Directions:

1. In a bowl, mix together all ingredients except for chicken drumsticks and lettuce.

2. Rub the chicken with the oil mix and refrigerate to marinate for about 20-30 minutes.

3. Arrange the chicken drumsticks into the greased air fry basket.

4. Select "Air Fry" of Breville Smart Air Fryer Oven and adjust the temperature to 390 degrees F.

5. Set the timer for 10 minutes and press "Start/Stop" to begin preheating.

6. When the unit beeps to show that it is preheated, insert the air fry basket in the oven.

7. After 10 minutes of cooking, set the temperature to 300 degrees F for 10 minutes.

8. When the cooking time is completed, remove the air fry basket from the oven and serve hot alongside the lettuce.

Cauliflower Patties

Servings: 4

Preparation Time: 10 minutes

Cooking Time 20 minutes

Ingredients:

- 3 large eggs
- 3 cups cauliflower florets
- ½ cup all-purpose flour
- 3 tbsp. wheat flour
- 1 tsp. coconut oil (melted)
- ½ tsp. garlic powder
- ½ tsp. turmeric
- ½ tsp. parsley
- Salt & pepper to taste
- Cooking oil spray

Directions:

1. Grate the cauliflower in a food processor then add parsley, turmeric, garlic powder, and wheat flour.

2. Whisk in eggs, and coconut oil then mix well.

3. Make 4 patties out of this cauliflower mixture and place them in the Air Fryer basket.

4. Set the Air Fryer basket inside the Air Fryer toaster oven and close the lid.

5. Select the Air Fry mode at 375°F temperature for 20 minutes.

6. Serve warm.

Spicy Chicken Legs

Servings: 6

Preparation Time: 15 minutes

Cooking Time: 25 minutes

Ingredients:

- 2½ pounds chicken legs
- 2 tablespoons olive oil
- 1 teaspoon smoked paprika
- 1 teaspoon garlic powder
- ½ teaspoon ground cumin
- Salt and ground black pepper, as required
- 8 cups fresh baby greens

Directions:

1. In a large bowl, add all the ingredients except for baby greens and mix well.

2. Arrange the chicken legs onto the greased enamel roasting pan.

3. Select "Air Fry" of Breville Smart Air Fryer Oven and adjust the temperature to 400 degrees F.

4. Set the timer for 25 minutes and press "Start/Stop" to begin preheating.

5. When the unit beeps to show that it is preheated, insert the roasting pan in the oven.

6. When the cooking time is completed, remove the roasting pan from the oven and transfer the chicken pieces onto a platter.

7. Serve hot alongside the baby greens.

Chicken with Mushrooms

Servings: 6

Preparation Time: 15 minutes

Cooking Time: 8 hours 10 minutes

Ingredients:

- 1 tablespoon olive oil
- 6 skinless, boneless chicken breasts
- 4 cups fresh button mushrooms, sliced
- 1 cup low-sodium chicken broth
- Salt and ground black pepper, as required

Directions:

1. In a skillet, heat the oil over medium heat and cook the chicken breasts for about 5 minutes per side.

2. Remove from the heat.

3. In an oven-safe pan that will fit in the Breville Smart Air Fryer Oven, place the chicken breasts and remaining ingredients and stir to combine.

4. Cover the pan with a lid.

5. Arrange the pan over the wire rack.

6. Select "Slow Cooker" of Breville Smart Air Fryer Oven and set on "Low".

7. Set the timer for 7-8 hours and press "Start/Stop" to begin cooking.

8. When the cooking time is completed, remove the pan from the oven and serve hot.

Panko Tofu with Mayo Sauce

Servings: 4

Preparation Time: 10 minutes

Cooking Time 20 minutes

Ingredients:

- 8 tofu cutlets

For the Marinade

- 1 tbsp toasted sesame oil 1/4 cup soy sauce
- 1 tsp rice vinegar
- 1/2 tsp garlic powder
- 1 tsp. ground ginger

Make the Tofu:

- 1/2 cup vegan mayo
- 1 cup panko breadcrumbs
- 1 tsp. of sea salt

Directions:

Whisk the marinade ingredients in a bowl and add tofu cutlets. Mix well to coat the cutlets. Cover and marinate for 1 hour. Meanwhile, whisk crumbs with salt and mayo in a bowl. Coat the cutlets with crumbs mixture. Place the tofu cutlets in the Air Fryer basket. Set the basket inside the Air Fryer toaster oven and close the lid. Select the Air Fry mode at 370°F temperature for 20 minutes. Flip the cutlets after 10 minutes then resume cooking. Serve warm.

Thyme Duck Breast

Servings: 2

Preparation Time: 10 minutes

Cooking Time: 20 minutes

Ingredients:

- 1 cup low-sodium chicken broth
- 2 tablespoons fresh lime juice
- 1 tablespoon olive oil
- 1 teaspoon mustard
- 1 tablespoon fresh thyme, chopped
- Salt and ground black pepper, as required
- 1 (10½-ounce) duck breast
- 3 cups fresh baby kale

Directions:

1. in a bowl, place the broth,, lime juice, oil, mustard, thyme, salt, and black pepper and mix well

2. Add the duck breast and coat with marinade generously.

3. Cover the bowl and refrigerate for about 4 hours.

4. Remove from the refrigerator and with a piece of foil, cover the duck breast.

5. Arrange the foil cover duck breast into the air fry basket.

6. Select "Air Fry" of Breville Smart Air Fryer Oven and adjust the temperature to 390 degrees F.

7. Set the timer for 15 minutes and press "Start/Stop" to begin preheating.

8. When the unit beeps to show that it is preheated, insert the air fry basket in the oven.

9. When the cooking time is completed, remove the air fry basket from the oven.

10. Remove the foil from the duck breast and again arrange in the air fry basket.

11. Select "Air Fry" of Breville Smart Air Fryer Oven and adjust the temperature to 355 degrees F.

12. Set the timer for 5 minutes and press "Start/Stop" to begin cooking.

13. When the cooking time is completed, remove the air fry basket from the oven and place the duck breast onto a cutting board for about 5 minutes before slicing.

14. With a sharp knife, cut the duck breast into desired size slices and serve alongside the kale.

Turkey with Carrots

Servings: 10

Preparation Time: 15 minutes

Cooking Time: 1¼ hours

Ingredients:

- ¼ cup olive oil
- 5 carrots, peeled and cut into chunks
- 1 (6-pound) boneless turkey breast
- Salt and ground black pepper, as required
- 1 cup low-sodium chicken broth

Directions:

1. In a pan, heat the oil over medium heat and cook the carrots for about 4-5 minutes.

2. Add the turkey breast and cook for about 10 minutes or until golden brown from both sides.

3. Remove from the heat and stir in salt, black pepper and broth.

4. Transfer the mixture into a baking dish.

5. Select "Bake" of Breville Smart Air Fryer Oven and adjust the temperature to 375 degrees F.

6. Set the timer for 60 minutes and press "Start/Stop" to begin preheating.

7. When the unit beeps to show that it is preheated, arrange the baking dish over the wire rack.

8. When the cooking time is completed, remove the baking dish from oven.

9. With tongs, place the turkey onto a cutting board for about 5 minutes before slicing.

10. Cut into desired-sized slices and serve alongside carrots.

Lemony Chicken Thighs

Servings: 6
Preparation Time: 15 minutes
Cooking Time: 20 minutes
Ingredients:

- 6 (6-ounce) chicken thighs
- 2 tablespoons olive oil
- 2 tablespoons fresh lemon juice
- 1 tablespoon Italian seasoning
- Salt and ground black pepper, as required
- 10 cups fresh arugula

Directions:

1. In a large bowl, add all the ingredients except for arugula and toss to coat well.

2. Refrigerate to marinate for 30 minutes to overnight.

3. Remove the chicken thighs from bowl and let any excess marinade drip off.

4. Arrange the chicken thighs onto the greased air fry basket.

5. Select "Air Fry" of Breville Smart Air Fryer Oven and adjust the temperature to 350 degrees F.

6. Set the timer for 20 minutes and press "Start/Stop" to begin preheating.

7. When the unit beeps to show that it is preheated, insert the air fry basket in the oven.

8. Flip the chicken thighs once halfway through.

9. When the cooking time is completed, remove the air fry basket from the oven and transfer the chicken thighs onto serving plates.

10. Serve hot alongside the arugula.

Tilapia Fish Sticks

Servings: 4
Preparation Time: 10 minutes
Cooking Time 15 minutes
Ingredients:

- 4 frozen tilapia fillets, cut into sticks
- 1 cup all-purpose flour
- 2 large eggs, beaten
- 1 1/2 cups seasoned panko breadcrumbs
- 1 tbsp. kosher salt
- For serving:
- 1 lemon, cut in wedges
- Tartar sauce
- Ketchup

Directions:

1. Mix flour with salt and dredge the tilapia sticks through the flour, then dip them in the egg and finally coat with the crumb's mixture.

2. Place the coated sticks in the Air Fryer basket.

3. Set the basket inside the Air Fryer toaster oven and close the lid.

4. Select the Air Fry mode at 390°F temperature for 12 minutes.

5. Serve with lemon wedges, tartar sauce, and ketchup.

Bacon-Wrapped Scallops

Servings: 9
Preparation Time: 10 minutes
Cooking Time 12 minutes
Ingredients:

- ½ cup mayonnaise
- 2 tbsp. Sriracha sauce
- 1-pound bay scallops
- 1 pinch coarse salt
- 1 pinch freshly cracked black pepper
- 12 slices bacon, cut into three pieces Olive oil cooking spray

Directions:

1. Whisk Sriracha sauce with mayonnaise in a bowl and keep it aside.

2. Place the scallops on the working surface and pat them dry.

3.   Sprinkle some salt, and black pepper on top, then wrap the 1/3 of a bacon slice around the scallops and secure it by inserting a toothpick.

4.   Place the scallops on the Air Fryer basket.

5.   Put the basket inside the Air Fryer toaster oven and close the lid.

6.   Select the Air Fry mode at 390°F temperature for 7 minutes. Serve warm with mayo sauce.

Turkey Rolls

Servings: 3

Preparation Time: 20 minutes

Cooking Time: 40 minutes

Ingredients:

- 1-pound turkey breast fillet
- 1 garlic clove, crushed
- 1½ teaspoons ground cumin
- 1 teaspoon ground cinnamon
- ½ teaspoon red chili powder
- Salt, as required
- 2 tablespoons olive oil
- 3 tablespoons fresh parsley, chopped finely
- 1 small red onion, chopped finely
- 4 cups fresh baby spinach

Directions:

1. Place the turkey fillet on a cutting board.

2. Carefully cut horizontally along the length about 1/3 of the way from the top, stopping about ¼-inch from the edge.

3. Open this part to have a long piece of fillet.

4. In a bowl, mix together the garlic, spices and oil.

5. In a small cup, reserve about 1 tablespoon of oil mixture.

6. In the remaining oil mixture, add the parsley and onion and mix well.

7. Coat the open side of fillet with onion mixture.

8. Roll the fillet tightly from the short side.

9. With a kitchen string, tie the roll at 1-1½-inch intervals.

10. Coat the outer side of roll with the reserved oil mixture.

11. Select "Air Fry" of Breville Smart Air Fryer Oven and adjust the temperature to 355 degrees F.

12. Set the timer for 40 minutes and press "Start/Stop" to begin preheating.

13. When the unit beeps to show that it is preheated, arrange the baking dish over the wire rack.

14. When the cooking time is completed, remove the baking dish from oven and place the turkey roll onto a cutting board for about 5-10 minutes before slicing.

15. With a sharp knife, cut the turkey roll into desired sized slices and serve alongside the spinach.

Parmesan Chicken Breasts

Servings: 2

Preparation Time: 15 minutes

Cooking Time: 22 minutes

Ingredients:

- 2 (6-ounce) chicken breasts
- 1 egg, beaten
- 4 ounces breadcrumbs
- 1 tablespoon fresh basil
- 2 tablespoons olive oil
- ¼ cup sugar-free pasta sauce
- ¼ cup low-fat Parmesan cheese, grated
- 3 cups fresh baby arugula

Directions:

1. In a shallow bowl, beat the egg.

2. In another bowl, add the oil, breadcrumbs, and basil and mix until a crumbly mixture forms.

3. Now, dip each chicken breast into the beaten egg and then coat with the breadcrumb mixture.

4. Arrange the chicken breasts into the greased air fry basket.

5. Select "Air Fry" of Breville Smart Air Fryer Oven and adjust the temperature to 350 degrees F.

6. Set the timer for 22 minutes and press "Start/Stop" to begin preheating.

7. When the unit beeps to show that it is preheated, insert the air fry basket in the oven.

8. After 15 minutes of cooking, spoon the pasta sauce over chicken breasts, followed by the cheese.

9. When the cooking time is completed, remove the air fry basket from the oven and transfer the chicken breasts onto serving plates.

10. Serve hot alongside the arugula.

Honey Graham Crackers

Servings: 48

Preparation Time: 10 minutes

Cooking Time 45 minutes

Ingredients:

- 2 Cups self-rising flour
- 1 Cup almond flour
- 1 Teaspoon baking powder
- ½ Cup butter, softened
- ½ Cup packed brown sugar ⅓ Cup honey
- 1 Teaspoon vanilla extract
- ½ Cup coconut milk

Directions:

1. Sieve self-rising flour, almond flour, baking powder and baking powder; keep separately.

2. In a medium container, butter, brown sugar and honey stir gently and loosely.

3. Add the sifted ingredients alternately with milk and vanilla.

4. Cover the dough and cool it overnight.

5. Preheat the Air fryer toaster oven to 175°C.

6. Divide the cold dough into quarters.

7. Spread the dough on a well-floured surface quarterly in a 5 x 15-inch rectangle.

8. Divide into rectangles with a knife.

9. Place rectangles on non-greased baking sheets.

10. Draw a line in the middle and click with a fork.

11. For a cinnamon biscuit, sprinkle with a mixture of sugar and cinnamon before baking.

12. Bake in the preheated oven for 13 to 15 minutes.

13. Remove the baking trays to cool them on racks.

Breaded Chicken Tenderloins

Servings: 4

Preparation Time: 15 minutes

Cooking Time: 15 minutes

Ingredients:

- 1 egg, beaten
- 2 tablespoons vegetable oil ½ cup breadcrumbs
- 8 skinless, boneless chicken tenderloins
- 6 cups fresh baby greens

Directions:

1. In a shallow dish, beat the egg.

1. In another dish, add the oil and breadcrumbs and mix until a crumbly mixture forms.

2. Dip the chicken tenderloins into beaten egg and then coat with the breadcrumbs mixture.

3. Shake off the excess coating.

4. Arrange the chicken tenderloins into the greased air fry basket.

5. Select "Air Fry" of Breville Smart Air Fryer Oven and adjust the temperature to 355 degrees F.

6. Set the timer for 15 minutes and press "Start/Stop" to begin preheating.

7. When the unit beeps to show that it is preheated, insert the air fry basket in the oven.

8. When the cooking time is completed, remove the air fry basket from the oven and serve hot alongside the greens.

Glazed Flat Iron Steak

Servings: 4

Preparation Time: 10 minutes

Cooking Time: 8 minutes

Ingredients:

- 1¼ pounds flat iron steak
- ½ cup low-sodium soy sauce ¼ cup fresh limes juice
- 2 tablespoons sesame oil
- 2 tablespoons honey
- 1 tablespoon red pepper flakes, crushed
- 2 garlic cloves, minced
- 6 cups lettuce, torn

Directions:

1. In a large resealable bag, place all the ingredients except for the lettuce.

2. Seal the bag and shake to mix well.

3. Refrigerate for up to 2 hours.

4. Remove the steak from bag and set aside at room temperature for 20 minutes before cooking.

5. Arrange the steak into the greased air fry basket.

6. Select "Bake" of Breville Smart Air Fryer Oven and adjust the temperature to 400 degrees F.

7. Set the timer for 8 minutes and press "Start/Stop" to begin preheating.

8. When the unit beeps to show that it is preheated, insert the air fry basket in the oven.

9. When the cooking time is completed, remove the air fry basket from the oven and place the steak onto a cutting board for about 10 minutes before slicing.

10. With a sharp knife, cut the steak into desired size slices and serve alongside the lettuce.

Balsamic Beef Top Roast

Servings: 10

Preparation Time: 10 minutes

Cooking Time: 45 minutes

Ingredients:

- 1 tablespoon coconut oil, melted
- 1 tablespoon balsamic vinegar
- ½ teaspoon ground cumin
- ½ teaspoon smoked paprika
- ½ teaspoon red pepper flakes, crushed
- Salt and ground black pepper, as required
- 3 pounds beef top roast
- 0 cups fresh baby greens

Directions:

1. In a bowl, add coconut oil, vinegar, spices, salt and black pepper and mix well.

2. Coat the roast with spice mixture generously.

3. With kitchen twines, tie the roast to keep it compact.

4. Arrange the roast onto the enamel roasting pan.

5. Select "Air Fry" of Breville Smart Air Fryer Oven and adjust the temperature to 360 degrees F.

6. Set the timer for 45 minutes and press "Start/Stop" to begin preheating.

7. When the unit beeps to show that it is preheated, insert the roasting pan in the oven.

8. When the cooking time is completed, remove the roasting pan from the oven and place the roast onto a cutting board for about 10 minutes before slicing.

9. With a sharp knife, cut the roast into desired sized slices and serve alongside the baby greens.

Spiced Chicken Breasts

Servings: 2

Preparation Time: 10 minutes

Cooking Time: 35 minutes

Ingredients:

- 1½ tablespoons smoked paprika
- 1 teaspoon ground cumin
- Salt and ground black pepper, as required
- 2 (12-ounce) bone-in, skin-on chicken breasts
- 1 tablespoon olive oil
- 3 cups fresh salad greens

Directions:

1. In a small bowl, mix together the paprika, cumin, salt and black pepper.

2. Coat the chicken breasts with oil evenly and then season with the spice mixture generously.

3. Arrange the chicken breasts into the greased air fry basket.

4. Select "Air Fry" of Breville Smart Air Fryer Oven and adjust the temperature to 375 degrees F.

5. Set the timer for 35 minutes and press "Start/Stop" to begin preheating.

6. When the unit beeps to show that it is preheated, insert the air fry basket in the oven.

7. Flip the chicken thighs once halfway through.

8. When the cooking time is completed, remove the air fry basket from the oven and transfer the chicken breasts onto a cutting board.

9. Cut each breast into 2 equal-sized pieces and serve alongside the greens.

Garlicky Pork Tenderloin

Servings: 5

Preparation Time: 15 minutes

Cooking Time: 20 minutes

Ingredients:

- 1½ pounds pork tenderloin
- Nonstick cooking spray
- 2 small heads roasted garlic
- Salt and ground black pepper, as required
- 8 cups fresh baby kale

Directions:

1. Lightly spray all the sides of pork with cooking spray and then season with salt and black pepper.

2. Now, rub the pork with roasted garlic.

3. Arrange the roast onto the lightly greased enamel roasting pan.

4. Select "Air Fry" of Breville Smart Air Fryer Oven and adjust the temperature to 400 degrees F.

5. Set the timer for 20 minutes and press "Start/Stop" to begin preheating.

6. When the unit beeps to show that it is preheated, insert the roasting pan in the oven.

7. Flip the side of tenderloin once halfway through.

8. When the cooking time is completed, remove the roasting pan from the oven and place the tenderloin onto a platter for about 10 minutes before slicing.

9. With a sharp knife, cut the roast into desired sized slices and serve alongside the kale.

Herbed Chicken Thighs

Servings: 4
Preparation Time: 10 minutes
Cooking Time: 20 minutes
Ingredients:
- ½ tablespoon fresh rosemary, minced
- ½ tablespoon fresh thyme, minced
- Salt and ground black pepper, as required
- 4 (5-ounce) chicken thighs
- 2 tablespoons olive oil
- 6 cups fresh baby spinach

Directions:

1. In a large bowl, add the herbs, salt and black pepper and mix well.

2. Coat the chicken thighs with oil and then rub with herb mixture.

3. Arrange the chicken thighs onto the greased enamel roasting pan.

4. Select "Air Fry" of Breville Smart Air Fryer Oven and adjust the temperature to 400 degrees F.

5. Set the timer for 20 minutes and press "Start/Stop" to begin preheating.

6. When the unit beeps to show that it is preheated, insert the roasting pan in the oven.

7. Flip the chicken thighs once halfway through.

8. When the cooking time is completed, remove the roasting pan from the oven and transfer the chicken thighs onto serving plates.

9. Serve hot alongside the spinach.

Beef & Veggie Kebabs

Servings: 4
Preparation Time: 15 minutes
Cooking Time: 12 minutes
Ingredients:
- ¼ cup low-sodium soy sauce ¼ cup olive oil
- 1 tablespoon garlic, minced
- 1 teaspoon brown sugar
- ½ teaspoon ground cumin
- Salt and ground black pepper, as required
- 1-pound sirloin steak, cut into-inch chunks
- 8 ounces baby Bella mushrooms, stems removed
- 1 large bell pepper, seeded and cut into 1-inch pieces
- 1 red onion, cut into 1-inch pieces

Directions:

1. In a bowl, mix together the soy sauce, oil, garlic, brown sugar, cumin, salt, and black pepper.

2. Add the steak cubes and coat with marinade generously.

3. Refrigerate to marinate for about 30 minutes.

4. Thread the steak cubes, mushrooms, bell pepper, and onion onto metal skewers.

5. Arrange the skewers into the greased air fry basket.

6. Select "Air Fry" of Breville Smart Air Fryer Oven and adjust the temperature to 390 degrees F.

7. Set the timer for 12 minutes and press "Start/Stop" to begin preheating.

8. When the unit beeps to show that it is preheated, insert the air fry basket in the oven.

9. When the cooking time is completed, remove the air fry basket from the oven and serve hot.

Beef, Spinach & Tomato Curry

Servings: 8
Preparation Time: 15 minutes
Cooking Time: 5 hours
Ingredients:

- 2 pounds boneless beef, cubed
- ½ cup fresh tomatoes, chopped finely 1¼ cups fresh spinach, chopped
- 2 cups low-sodium beef broth
- 1 cup unsweetened coconut milk
- Salt and ground black pepper, as required

Directions:

1. In an oven-safe pan that will fit in the Breville Smart Air Fryer Oven, place all ingredients and stir to combine.

2. Cover the pan with a lid.

3. Arrange the pan over the wire rack.

4. Select "Slow Cooker" of Breville Smart Air Fryer Oven and set on "High".

5. Set the timer for 5 hours and press "Start/Stop" to begin cooking.

6. When the cooking time is completed, remove the pan from the oven.

7. Remove the lid and stir the mixture well.

8. Serve hot.

Spiced Flank Steak

Servings: 6

Preparation Time: 10 minutes

Cooking Time: 12 minutes

Ingredients:

- 2 tablespoons balsamic vinegar
- 2 tablespoons olive oil
- 3 garlic cloves, minced
- 1 teaspoon red chili powder
- 1 teaspoon ground cumin
- 1 teaspoon onion powder
- Salt and ground black pepper, as required
- 1 (2-pound) flank steak
- 8 cups fresh baby kale

Directions:

1. In a large bowl, mix together the vinegar, spices, salt and black pepper.

2. Add the steak and coat with mixture generously.

3. Cover the bowl and place in the refrigerator for at least 1 hour.

4. Remove the steak from bowl and place onto the greased enamel roasting pan.

5. Select "Broil" of Breville Smart Air Fryer Oven and set the timer for 12 minutes.

6. Press "Start/Stop" to begin preheating.

7. When the unit beeps to show that it is preheated, insert the roasting pan in the oven.

8. When the cooking time is completed, remove the roasting pan from the oven and place the steak onto a cutting board.

9. With a sharp knife, cut the steak into desired sized slices and serve alongside the baby kale.

Ground Turkey with Olives

Servings: 8

Preparation Time: 15 minutes

Cooking Time: 4 hours 10 minutes

Ingredients:

- 1 teaspoon olive oil
- 2½ pounds ground turkey
- 1 cup red bell peppers, chopped
- 1 cup onion, minced
- 3 cloves garlic, minced
- ¼ cup fresh cilantro, minced
- 1 small tomato, chopped
- 8 ounces canned tomato sauce
- ¼ cup green olives, pitted
- 2 bay leaves
- 1½ teaspoons ground cumin
- ¼ teaspoon garlic powder
- Salt and ground black pepper, as required 1¼ cups water

Directions:

1. In a Dutch oven that will fit in the Breville Smart Air Fryer Oven, heat the oil over medium heat and cook the turkey with salt and black pepper for about 5-6 minutes.

2. Add the bell pepper, onion and garlic and cook for about 3-4 minutes.

3. Remove from the heat and stir in the remaining ingredients.

4. Arrange the Dutch oven over the wire rack.

5. Select "Slow Cooker" of Breville Smart Air Fryer Oven and set on "High".

6. Set the timer for 4 hours and press "Start/Stop" to begin cooking.

7. When the cooking time is completed, remove the Dutch oven from the oven.

8. Remove the lid and discard the bay leaves.

9. Serve hot.

Chicken with Zucchini & Asparagus

Servings: 8
Preparation Time: 20 minutes
Cooking Time: 8 hours 40 minutes
Ingredients:

- 2 pounds skinless, boneless chicken breast tenders
- 1 large onion, chopped
- 2 cups asparagus, trimmed and cut into 2-inch pieces
- 1 tablespoon fresh thyme, chopped
- 1 teaspoon garlic powder
- Salt and ground black pepper, as required
- 4 medium zucchinis, spiralized with blade C
- 1 cup low-fat cheddar cheese, shredded

Directions:

1. In an oven-safe pan that will fit in the Breville Smart Air Fryer Oven, In the pot of the chicken, onion, asparagus, thyme, garlic powder, salt and black pepper and mix well.

2. Cover the pan with a lid.

3. Arrange the pan over the wire rack.

4. Select "Slow Cooker" of Breville Smart Air Fryer Oven and set on "Low".

5. Set the timer for 8 hours and press "Start/Stop" to begin cooking.

6. When the cooking time is completed, remove the pan from the oven.

7. Open the lid and place the zucchini noodles over the chicken mixture.

8. Top with cheese evenly.

9. Cover the pan with a lid.

10. Arrange the pan over the wire rack.

11. Select "Slow Cooker" of Breville Smart Air Fryer Oven and set on "Low".

12. Set the timer for30-40 minutes and press "Start/Stop" to begin cooking.

13. When the cooking time is completed, remove the pan from the oven and serve hot.

Spiced Rib-Eye Steak

Servings: 6
Preparation Time: 10 minutes
Cooking Time: 14 minutes
Ingredients:

- ½ teaspoon ground cumin
- ½ teaspoon garlic powder
- ½ teaspoon paprika
- Salt and ground black pepper, as required
- 2 pounds rib-eye steak
- 1 tablespoon olive oil
- 8 cups fresh baby kale

Directions:

1. In a bowl, mix together the spices. Salt and black pepper.

2. Coat the steak with oil and then rub with spice mixture generously.

3. Arrange the steaks into the greased air fry basket.

4. Select "Air Fry" of Breville Smart Air Fryer Oven and adjust the temperature to 400 degrees F.

5. Set the timer for 14 minutes and press "Start/Stop" to begin preheating.

6. When the unit beeps to show that it is preheated, insert the air fry basket in the oven.

7. When the cooking time is completed, remove the air fry basket from the oven and place the steak onto a cutting board for about 10 minutes before slicing.

8. Cut the steak into desired sized slices and serve alongside the kale.

Beef & Mushroom Meatloaf

Servings: 4
Preparation Time: 15 minutes
Cooking Time: 25 minutes
Ingredients:

- 1-pound lean ground beef
- 1 small onion, finely chopped
- 1 tablespoon fresh thyme, finely chopped
- 3 tablespoons dry breadcrumbs
- 1 egg, lightly beaten
- Salt and ground black pepper, as required
- 2 mushrooms, thickly sliced
- 1 tablespoon olive oil

Directions:

1. In a bowl, add the beef, onion, thyme, breadcrumbs, egg, salt, and black pepper. With your hands, mix until well combined.

2. Place the beef mixture into a lightly greased baking pan and with the back of a spoon, smooth the top surface.

3. Arrange the mushroom slices on top and gently press each inside the meatloaf.

4. Coat the meatloaf with oil.

5. Arrange the baking pan into the greased air fry basket.

6. Select "Air Fry" of Breville Smart Air Fryer Oven and adjust the temperature to 392 degrees F.

7. Set the timer for 25 minutes and press "Start/Stop" to begin preheating.

8. When the unit beeps to show that it is preheated, insert the air fry basket in the oven.

9. When the cooking time is completed, remove the air fry basket from the oven and place the pan onto a wire rack for about 10 minutes before serving.

10. Cut into desired size wedges and serve.

Seasoned Rib-Eye Steak

Servings: 3

Preparation Time: 10 minutes

Cooking Time: 14 minutes

Ingredients:

- 2 (8-ounce) rib-eye steaks
- 2 tablespoons olive oil
- 1 tablespoon simple steak seasoning
- Salt and ground black pepper, as required
- 3 cups fresh salad greens

Directions:

1. Coat the steaks with oil and then sprinkle with seasoning, salt and black pepper evenly.

2. Arrange the steaks onto the enamel roasting pan.

3. Select "Bake" of Breville Smart Air Fryer Oven and adjust the temperature to 400 degrees F.

4. Set the timer for 14 minutes and press "Start/Stop" to begin preheating.

5. When the unit beeps to show that it is preheated, insert the roasting pan in the oven.

6. When the cooking time is completed, remove the roasting pan from the oven and place the steaks onto a cutting board for about 5 minutes.

7. Cut each steak into desired size slices and serve alongside the salad greens.

Lemony Salmon

Servings: 2

Preparation Time: 10 minutes

Cooking Time: 10 minutes

Ingredients:

- 1 tablespoon fresh lemon juice ½ tablespoons olive oil
- Salt and ground black pepper, as required
- 1 garlic clove, minced
- ½ teaspoon fresh thyme leaves, chopped
- 2 (7-ounce) salmon fillets
- 3 cups fresh salad greens

Directions:

1. In a bowl, add all the ingredients except the salmon and greens and mix well.

2. Add the salmon fillets and coat with the mixture generously.

3. Coat the fillets with flour mixture, then dip into egg mixture and finally coat with the cornflake mixture.

4. Arrange the salmon fillets onto a lightly greased wire rack, skin-side down.

5. Select "Air Fry" of Breville Smart Air Fryer Oven and adjust the temperature to 400 degrees F.

6. Set the timer for 10 minutes and press "Start/Stop" to begin preheating.

7. When the unit beeps to show that it is preheated, insert the wire rack in the oven.

8. Flip the salmon fillets once halfway through.

9. When the cooking time is completed, remove the salmon fillets from the oven and transfer onto serving plates.

10. Serve hot alongside the greens.

Simple Salmon

Servings: 2

Preparation Time: 10 minutes

Cooking Time: 10 minutes

Ingredients:

- 2 (6-ounce) salmon fillets
- Salt and ground black pepper, as required
- 1 tablespoon olive oil
- 3 cups fresh baby spinach

Directions:

1. Season each salmon fillet with salt and black pepper and then coat with the oil.

2. Arrange the salmon fillets into the greased air fry basket.

3. Select "Air Fry" of Breville Smart Air Fryer Oven and adjust the temperature to 360 degrees F.

4. Set the timer for 10 minutes and press "Start/Stop" to begin preheating.

5. When the unit beeps to show that it is preheated, insert the air fry basket in the oven.

6. When the cooking time is completed, remove the air fry basket from the oven and transfer the salmon fillets onto serving plates.

7. Serve hot alongside the spinach.

Seasoned Striploin Steak

Servings: 2

Preparation Time: 15 minutes

Cooking Time: 12 minutes

Ingredients:

- 2 (7-ounces) striploin steaks
- 1½ tablespoons olive oil
- Salt and ground black pepper, as required
- 1 tablespoon steak seasoning
- 3 cups fresh baby arugula

Directions:

1. Coat each steak evenly with oil and then season with salt and black pepper.

2. Now rub the steak with steak seasoning.

3. Arrange the steaks into the greased air fry basket.

4. Select "Air Fry" of Breville Smart Air Fryer Oven and adjust the temperature to 392 degrees F.

5. Set the timer for 12 minutes and press "Start/Stop" to begin preheating.

6. When the unit beeps to show that it is preheated, insert the air fry basket in the oven.

7. When the cooking time is completed, remove the air fry basket from the oven and serve hot alongside the arugula.

Pesto Salmon

Servings: 4

Preparation Time: 15 minutes

Cooking Time: 15 minutes

Ingredients:

For Salmon:

- 1¼ pounds salmon fillet, cut into 4 fillets
- 2 tablespoons fresh lemon juice
- 2 tablespoons pesto, thawed

For Serving:

- 1 cucumber, chopped
- 1 large tomato, chopped

Directions:

1. Arrange the salmon fillets onto a foil-lined baking dish, skin-side down.

2. Drizzle the salmon fillets with lemon juice.

3. Set aside for about 15 minutes.

4. Spread pesto over each salmon fillet evenly.

5. Arrange the salmon fillets into the greased baking dish.

6. Select "Broil" of Breville Smart Air Fryer Oven and then set the timer for 15 minutes.

7. Press "Start/Stop" to begin preheating.

8. When the unit beeps to show that it is preheated, arrange the baking dish over the wire rack.

9. When the cooking time is completed, remove the baking dish from oven and transfer the salmon fillets onto serving plates.

10. Serve hot alongside cucumber and tomato.

Beef & Mushroom Stuffed Bell Peppers

Servings: 4

Preparation Time: 20 minutes

Cooking Time: 26 minutes

Ingredients:

- 1 teaspoon olive oil
- ½ medium onion, chopped
- ½ cup fresh mushrooms, chopped finely
- 2 garlic cloves, minced
- 1-pound lean ground beef
- 1 teaspoon dried basil, crushed
- 1 teaspoon garlic salt
- ½ teaspoon red chili powder
- Ground black pepper, as required
- 2/3 cup low-fat Mexican cheese, shredded and divided
- 8 ounces tomato sauce, divided
- 2 teaspoons Worcestershire sauce
- 4 bell peppers, tops removed and seeded

Directions:

1. In a medium skillet, heat oil over medium heat and sauté the onion, mushroom and garlic

for about 3-5 minutes or until cooked thoroughly.

2. Add the ground beef, basil, and spices. Cook for about 8-10 minutes.

3. Remove the skillet from heat and drain off the excess grease from skillet.

4. Add half of the cheese, 2/3 of the tomato sauce and Worcestershire sauce and mix until well combined.

5. Stuff each bell pepper with beef mixture evenly.

6. Arrange the bell peppers into the greased air fry basket.

7. Select "Air Fry" of Breville Smart Air Fryer Oven and adjust the temperature to 400 degrees F.

8. Set the timer for 11 minutes and press "Start/Stop" to begin preheating.

9. When the unit beeps to show that it is preheated, insert the air fry basket in the oven.

10. After 7 minutes of cooking, top each bell pepper with the remaining tomato sauce and cheese.

11. When the cooking time is completed, remove the air fry basket from the oven and serve hot.

Pork with Mushrooms

Servings: 5

Preparation Time: 15 minutes

Cooking Time: 4 hours

Ingredients:

- 1 yellow onion, sliced
- 1½ pounds pork tenderloin, cut into slices
- ½ pound fresh button mushrooms, sliced
- 2 tablespoons olive oil
- Salt and ground black pepper, as required
- 2 cups low-sodium chicken broth

Directions:

1. Lightly grease a Dutch oven that will fit in the Breville Smart Air Fryer Oven.

2. In the bottom of pot, arrange the onion slices and top with the pork tenderloin, followed by the mushroom slices.

3. Sprinkle with salt and black pepper and pour the broth on top.

4. Arrange the Dutch oven over the wire rack.

5. Select "Slow Cooker" of Breville Smart Air Fryer Oven and set on "High".

6. Set the timer for 4 hours and press "Start/Stop" to begin cooking.

7. When the cooking time is completed, remove the Dutch oven from the oven.

8. Open the lid and stir the mixture.

9. Serve hot.

Ground Beef with Olives

Servings: 8

Preparation Time: 15 minutes

Cooking Time: 4 hours 10 minutes

Ingredients:

- 1 teaspoon olive oil
- 2½ pounds ground beef
- 1 cup red bell peppers, chopped
- 1 cup onion, minced
- 3 cloves garlic, minced
- ¼ cup fresh cilantro, minced
- 1 small tomato, chopped
- 8 ounces canned tomato sauce
- ¼ cup green olives, pitted
- 2 bay leaves
- 1½ teaspoons ground cumin
- ¼ teaspoon garlic powder
- Salt and ground black pepper, as required
  1¼ cups water

Directions:

1. In a skillet, heat the oil over medium heat and cook the beef with salt and black pepper for about 5-6 minutes.

2. Add the bell pepper, onion and garlic and cook for about 3-4 minutes.

3. Remove from the heat and place the beef mixture into a baking dish.

4. Add the remaining ingredients and stir to combine.

5. Place the baking dish over wire rack.

6. Select "Slow Cooker" of Breville Smart Air Fryer Oven and set on "High".

7. Set the timer for 4 hours and press "Start/Stop" to begin cooking.

8. When the cooking time is completed, remove the baking dish from the oven and discard the bay leaves.

9. Serve hot.

Maple Pork Tenderloin

Servings: 3

Preparation Time: 10 minutes

Cooking Time: 20 minutes

Ingredients:

*   2 tablespoons Sriracha
*   2 tablespoons maple syrup
*   ¼ teaspoon red pepper flakes, crushed Salt, as required
*   1-pound pork tenderloin
*   5 cups fresh baby greens

Directions:

1. In a small bowl, add the Sriracha, maple syrup, red pepper flakes and salt and mix well.

2. Arrange the pork tenderloin into the greased air fry basket.

3. Brush the pork tenderloin with mixture evenly.

4. Select "Air Fry" of Breville Smart Air Fryer Oven and adjust the temperature to 350 degrees F.

5. Set the timer for 20 minutes and press "Start/Stop" to begin preheating.

6. When the unit beeps to show that it is preheated, insert the air fry basket in the oven.

7. When the cooking time is completed, remove the air fry basket from the oven and placethe pork tenderloin onto a platter for about 10 minutes before slicing.

8. With a sharp knife, cut the roast into desired sized slices and serve alongside the greens.

Pork with Green Beans

Servings: 3

Preparation Time: 15 minutes

Cooking Time: 13 minutes

Ingredients:

*   3 (6-ounces) pork tenderloins
*   2 tablespoons olive oil
*   Salt and ground black pepper, as required ¾ pound frozen green beans

Directions:

1. Coat the pork tenderloins with oil and then rub with salt and black pepper.

2. Arrange the pork tenderloins into the greased air fry basket.

3. Select "Air Fry" of Breville Smart Air Fryer Oven and adjust the temperature to 392 degrees F.

4. Set the timer for 12 minutes and press "Start/Stop" to begin preheating.

5. When the unit beeps to show that it is preheated, insert the air fry basket in the oven.

6. After 6 minutes of cooking, arrange the green beans around the tenderloins.

7. When the cooking time is completed, remove the air fry basket from the oven and place the pork tenderloins onto a platter.

8. Cut each tenderloin into desired sized slices and serve alongside the green beans.

Sweet & Sour Salmon

Servings: 2

Preparation Time: 10 minutes

Cooking Time: 13 minutes

Ingredients:

*   3 tablespoons low-sodium soy sauce
*   2 tablespoons maple syrup
*   2 teaspoons fresh lemon juice
*   2 teaspoons water
*   2 (4-ounce) salmon fillets
*   3 cups fresh arugula

Directions:

1. In a small bowl, place all the ingredients except the salmon and arugula and mix well.

2. In a small bowl, reserve about half of the mixture.

3. Add the salmon in the remaining mixture and coat well.

4. Refrigerate, covered to marinate for about 2 hours.

5. Arrange the salmon fillets into the greased air fry basket.

6. Select "Air Fry" of Breville Smart Air Fryer Oven and adjust the temperature to 355 degrees F.

7. Set the timer for 13 minutes and press "Start/Stop" to begin preheating.

8. When the unit beeps to show that it is preheated, insert the air fry basket in the oven.

9. After 8 minutes, flip the salmon fillets and coat with reserved marinade.

10. When the cooking time is completed, remove the air fry basket from the oven and serve hot alongside the arugula.

Cod Burgers

Servings: 6
Preparation Time: 15 minutes
Cooking Time: 7 minutes
Ingredients:
* 1-pound cod fillet
* 1 teaspoon fresh lime zest, finely grated
* 1 egg
* 1 teaspoon red chili paste Salt, as required
* 1 tablespoon fresh lime juice
* 1/3 cup coconut, grated and divided
* 1 scallion, finely chopped
* 2 tablespoons fresh parsley, chopped
* 8 cups fresh baby greens
* 1 cup cherry tomatoes, halved

Directions:
1. For cod patties: in a food processor, add the cod fillet, lime zest, egg, chili paste, salt, and lime juice and pulse until smooth.

2. Transfer the cod mixture into a bowl.

3. Add 2 tablespoons of coconut, scallion, and parsley and mix until well combined.

4. Make 12 equal-sized patties from the mixture.

5. In a shallow bowl, place the remaining coconut.

6. Coat the cod patties with coconut evenly.

7. Arrange the patties into the greased air fry basket.

8. Select "Air Fry" of Breville Smart Air Fryer Oven and adjust the temperature to 375 degrees F.

9. Set the timer for 7 minutes and press "Start/Stop" to begin preheating.

10. When the unit beeps to show that it is preheated, insert the air fry basket in the oven.

11. When the cooking time is completed, remove the air fry basket from the oven and serve alongside the greens and tomatoes.

Spiced Tilapia

Servings: 2
Preparation Time: 10 minutes
Cooking Time: 12 minutes
Ingredients:
* ½ teaspoon lemon pepper seasoning ½ teaspoon garlic powder
* 1/2 teaspoon onion powder
* Salt and ground black pepper, as required
* 2 (6-ounce) tilapia fillets
* 1 tablespoon olive oil
* 3 cups fresh spinach

Directions:
1. In a small bowl, mix together the spices, salt and black pepper.

2. Coat the tilapia fillets with oil and then rub with spice mixture.

3. Arrange the tilapia fillets onto a lightly greased wire rack, skin-side down.

4. Select "Air Fry" of Breville Smart Air Fryer Oven and adjust the temperature to 360 degrees F.

5. Set the timer for 12 minutes and press "Start/Stop" to begin preheating.

6. When the unit beeps to show that it is preheated, insert the wire rack in the oven.

7. Flip the tilapia fillets once hallway through.

8. When the cooking time is completed, remove the tilapia fillets from the oven and transfer onto serving plates.

9. Serve hot alongside the spinach.

Salmon with Asparagus

Servings: 2
Preparation Time: 15 minutes
Cooking Time: 11 minutes
Ingredients:
* 2 (6-ounces) boneless salmon fillets
* 1½ tablespoons fresh lemon juice
* 1 tablespoon olive oil
* 2 tablespoons fresh parsley, roughly chopped
* 2 tablespoons fresh dill, roughly chopped
* 1 bunch asparagus
* Salt and ground black pepper, as required

Directions:
1. In a small bowl, mix well the lemon juice, oil, herbs, salt, and black pepper.

2. In another large bowl, mix together the salmon and ¾ of oil mixture.

3. In a second large bowl, add the asparagus and remaining oil mixture and mix well.

4. Arrange the asparagus into the greased air fry basket.

5. Select "Air Fry" of Breville Smart Air Fryer Oven and adjust the temperature to 400 degrees F.

6. Set the timer for 11 minutes and press "Start/Stop" to begin preheating.

7. When the unit beeps to show that it is preheated, insert the air fry basket in the oven.

8. After 3 minutes of cooking, place the salmon fillets on top of the asparagus

9. When the cooking time is completed, remove the air fry basket from the oven and serve hot.

Beef & Chedar Burgers

Servings: 2

Preparation Time: 15 minutes

Cooking Time: 12 minutes

Ingredients:

- ½ pound ground beef
- 1 garlic clove, minced
- 2 tablespoons fresh cilantro, minced
- Salt and ground black pepper, as required
- 2 low-fat cheddar cheese slices
- 4 cups lettuce, torn
- 1 cup grape tomatoes, halved

Directions:

1. In a bowl, mix together the beef, garlic, cilantro, salt, and black pepper.

2. Make 2 (4-inch) patties from the mixture.

3. Arrange the patties into the greased air fry basket.

4. Select "Air Fry" of Breville Smart Air Fryer Oven and adjust the temperature to 390 degrees F.

5. Set the timer for 12 minutes and press "Start/Stop" to begin preheating.

6. When the unit beeps to show that it is preheated, insert the air fry basket in the oven.

7. After 11 minutes of cooking, place 1 cheese slice over each patty.

8. When the cooking time is completed, remove the air fry basket from the oven and serve hot alongside the lettuce and tomatoes.

BBQ Pork Chops

Servings: 4

Preparation Time: 10 minutes

Cooking Time: 16 minutes

Ingredients:

- 4 (8-ounce) pork loin chops
- Salt and ground black pepper, as required ½ cup sugar-free BBQ sauce
- 6 cups fresh salad greens

Directions:

1. With a meat mallet, pound the chops completely.

2. Sprinkle the chops with a little salt and black pepper.

3. In a large bowl, add the BBQ sauce and chops and mix well.

4. Refrigerate, covered for about 6-8 hours.

5. Remove the chops from bowl and discard the excess sauce.

6. Arrange the chops into the greased air fry basket.

7. Select "Air Fry" of Breville Smart Air Fryer Oven and adjust the temperature to 355 degrees F.

8. Set the timer for 16 minutes and press "Start/Stop" to begin preheating.

9. When the unit beeps to show that it is preheated, insert the air fry basket in the oven.

10. Flip the chops once halfway through.

11. When the cooking time is completed, remove the air fry basket from the oven and serve alongside the greens.

Salmon with Broccoli

Servings: 2

Preparation Time: 15 minutes

Cooking Time: 12 minutes

Ingredients:

- 1½ cups small broccoli florets
- 2 tablespoons vegetable oil, divided
- Salt and ground black pepper, as required
- 1 (½-inch) piece fresh ginger, grated
- 1 tablespoon soy sauce
- 1 teaspoon balsamic vinegar
- 1 teaspoon Erythritol
- ¼ teaspoon arrowroot starch
- 2 (6-ounce) skin-on salmon fillets
- 1 scallion, thinly sliced

Directions:

1. In a bowl, mix together the broccoli, 1 tablespoon of oil, salt, and black pepper.

2. In another bowl, mix well the ginger, soy sauce, vinegar, Erythritol, and cornstarch.

3. Coat the salmon fillets with the remaining oil and then with the ginger mixture.

4. Arrange the broccoli florets into the greased air fry basket and top with the salmon fillets.

5. Select "Air Fry" of Breville Smart Air Fryer Oven and adjust the temperature to 375 degrees F.

6. Set the timer for 12 minutes and press "Start/Stop" to begin preheating.

7. When the unit beeps to show that it is preheated, insert the air fry basket in the oven.

8. When the cooking time is completed, remove the air fry basket from the oven and transfer the salmon fillets and broccoli onto serving plates.

9. Serve hot.

Cajun Catfish

Servings: 4

Preparation Time: 10 minutes

Cooking Time: 14 minutes

Ingredients:

- 2 tablespoons almond flour
- 2 teaspoons Cajun seasoning ½ teaspoon paprika
- ½ teaspoon garlic powder Salt, as required
- 2 (6-ounces) catfish fillets
- 1 tablespoon olive oil
- 6 cups fresh baby spinach

Directions:

1. In a bowl, mix together the flour, Cajun seasoning, paprika, garlic powder, and salt.

2. Add the catfish fillets and coat with the mixture evenly.

3. Now, coat each fillet with oil.

4. Arrange the fish fillets into the greased air fry basket.

5. Select "Air Fry" of Breville Smart Air Fryer Oven and adjust the temperature to 400 degrees F.

6. Set the timer for 14 minutes and press "Start/Stop" to begin preheating.

7. When the unit beeps to show that it is preheated, insert the air fry basket in the oven.

8. Flip the fish fillets once halfway through.

9. When the cooking time is completed, remove the air fry basket from the oven and serve hot alongside the spinach.

Pork Chili

Servings: 6

Preparation Time: 15 minutes

Cooking Time: 4 hours 10 minutes

Ingredients:

- ½ teaspoon olive oil
- 2 pounds lean ground pork
- 1 small onion, chopped
- 3 bell peppers, seeded and chopped
- 5 garlic cloves, minced
- 2 (14-ounce) cans sugar-free diced tomatoes 1½ cups low-sodium beef broth
- 2 tablespoons red chili powder
- ¼ teaspoon cayenne pepper
- ¼ teaspoon Italian seasoning
- Salt and ground black pepper, as required
- 1/3 cup low-fat cheddar cheese, shredded

Directions:

1. In an oven-safe pan that will fit in the Breville Smart Air Fryer Oven, heat the oil over medium heat and cook the pork for about 8-10 minutes.

2. Remove from the heat and stir in the remaining ingredients.

3. Cover the pan with a lid.

4. Arrange the pan over the wire rack.

5. Select "Slow Cooker" of Breville Smart Air Fryer Oven and set on "High".

6. Set the timer for 4 hours and press "Start/Stop" to begin cooking.

7. When the cooking time is completed, remove the pan from the oven.

8. Remove the lid and stir the mixture well.

9. Serve hot with the topping of cheddar cheese.

Feta Pork Meatballs

Servings: 8

Preparation Time: 20 minutes

Cooking Time: 24 minutes

Ingredients:

- 2 pounds ground pork
- 1 medium onion, chopped roughly
- ¼ cup fresh parsley, chopped roughly

- 4 garlic cloves, peeled
- ½ cup feta cheese, crumbled
- ½ cup Italian seasoned breadcrumbs
- 2 eggs, lightly beaten
- 1 tablespoon Worcestershire sauce
- Salt and ground black pepper, as required
- 12 cups fresh salad greens

Directions:

1. In a mini food processor, add the onion, parsley and garlic and pulse until finely chopped.

2. Transfer the onion mixture into a large bowl.

3. Add the remaining ingredients except for greens and mix until well combined.

4. Make equal-sized balls from the mixture.

5. Arrange the meatballs into the greased air fry basket in a single layer.

6. Select "Air Fry" of Breville Smart Air Fryer Oven and adjust the temperature to 400 degrees F.

7. Set the timer for 12 minutes and press "Start/Stop" to begin preheating.

8. When the unit beeps to show that it is preheated, insert the air fry basket in the oven.

9. When the cooking time is completed, remove the air fry basket from the oven and transfer the meatballs onto a platter.

10. Serve hot alongside the greens.

Shrimp with Tomatoes

Servings: 4

Preparation Time: 15 minutes

Cooking Time: 7¼ hours

Ingredients:

- 1 (14-ounce) can peeled tomatoes, chopped finely
- 4 ounces canned tomato paste
- 2 garlic cloves, minced
- 2 tablespoons fresh parsley, chopped
- Salt and ground black pepper, as required
- 1 teaspoon lemon pepper
- 2 pounds cooked shrimp, peeled and deveined

Directions:

1. In an oven-safe pan that will fit in the Breville Smart Air Fryer Oven, place all ingredients except for shrimp and stir to combine.

2. Cover the pan with a lid.

3. Arrange the pan over the wire rack.

4. Select "Slow Cooker" of Breville Smart Air Fryer Oven and set on "Low".

5. Set the timer for 7 hours and press "Start/Stop" to begin cooking.

6. When the cooking time is completed, remove the pan from the oven.

7. Remove the lid and stir in the shrimp.

8. Again arrange the pan over the wire rack.

9. Select "Slow Cooker" of Breville Smart Air Fryer Oven and set on "High".

10. Set the timer for 15 minutes and press "Start/Stop" to begin cooking.

11. When the cooking time is completed, remove the pan from the oven.

12. Remove the lid and stir and serve hot.

Tuna & Mustard Burgers

Servings: 4

Preparation Time: 15 minutes

Cooking Time: 6 minutes

Ingredients:

For Burgers:

- 7 ounces canned tuna
- 1 large egg
- ¼ cup breadcrumbs
- 1 tablespoon mustard
- ¼ teaspoon garlic powder
- ¼ teaspoon onion powder
- ¼ teaspoon cayenne pepper
- Salt and ground black pepper, as required

For Serving:

- 1 large cucumber, chopped
- 4 cups fresh baby spinach

Directions:

1. For burgers: in a bowl, add all the ingredients and mix until well combined.

2. Make 4 equal-sized patties from the mixture.

3. Arrange the patties onto the greased enamel roasting pan.

4. Select "Air Fry" of Breville Smart Air Fryer Oven and adjust the temperature to 400 degrees F.

5. Set the timer for 6 minutes and press "Start/Stop" to begin preheating.

6. When the unit beeps to show that it is preheated, insert the roasting pan in the oven.

7. Flip the burgers once halfway through.

8. When the cooking time is completed, remove the roasting pan from the oven and transfer the burgers onto serving plates.

9. Serve hot alongside the cucumber and spinach

Tangy Sea Bass

Servings: 2

Preparation Time: 10 minutes

Cooking Time: 12 minutes

Ingredients:

* 2 (5-ounce) sea bass fillets
* 1 garlic clove, minced
* 1 teaspoon fresh dill, minced
* 1 tablespoon olive oil
* 1 tablespoon balsamic vinegar
* Salt and ground black pepper, as required
* 2 cups fresh baby spinach

Directions:

1. In a large resealable bag, add all the ingredients.

2. Seal the bag and shale well to mix.

3. Refrigerate to marinate for at least 30 minutes.

4. Remove the fish fillets from bag and shake off the excess marinade.

5. Arrange the fish fillets onto the greased enamel roasting pan in a single layer.

6. Select "Bake" of Breville Smart Air Fryer Oven and adjust the temperature to 450 degrees F.

7. Set the timer for 12 minutes and press "Start/Stop" to begin preheating.

8. When the unit beeps to show that it is preheated, insert the roasting pan in the oven.

9. Flip the fish fillets once halfway through.

10. When the cooking time is completed, remove the roasting pan from the oven and transfer the fish fillets onto serving plates.

11. Serve hot alongside the spinach.

Simple Trout

Servings: 2

Preparation Time: 10 minutes

Cooking Time: 10 minutes

Ingredients:

* 2 (6-ounce) trout fillets

* Salt and ground black pepper, as required
* 1 tablespoon olive oil
* 4 cups fresh baby spinach

Directions:

1. Season each trout fillet with salt and black pepper and then coat with the oil.

2. Arrange the trout fillets onto the greased enamel roasting pan in a single layer.

3. Select "Air Fry" of Breville Smart Air Fryer Oven and adjust the temperature to 360 degrees F.

4. Set the timer for 10 minutes and press "Start/Stop" to begin preheating.

5. When the unit beeps to show that it is preheated, insert the roasting pan in the oven.

6. Flip the fillets once halfway through.

7. When the cooking time is completed, remove the roasting pan from the oven and transfer the trout fillets onto serving plates.

8. Serve hot alongside the spinach.

Scallops with Spinach

Servings: 2

Preparation Time: 15 minutes

Cooking Time: 10 minutes

Ingredients:

* 1 (12-ounces) package frozen spinach, thawed and drained
* 8 jumbo sea scallops
* Olive oil cooking spray
* Salt and ground black pepper, as required ¾ cup low-fat cream
* 1 tablespoon tomato paste
* 1 teaspoon garlic, minced
* 1 tablespoon fresh basil, chopped

Directions:

1. In the bottom of a 7-inch heatproof pan, place the spinach.

2. Spray each scallop evenly with cooking spray and then, sprinkle with a little salt and black pepper.

3. Arrange scallops on top of the spinach in a single layer.

4. In a bowl, add the cream, tomato paste, garlic, basil, salt, and black pepper and mix well.

5. Place the cream mixture over the spinach and scallops evenly.

6. Arrange the pan into the air fry basket.

7. Select "Air Fry" of Breville Smart Air Fryer Oven and adjust the temperature to 350 degrees F.

8. Set the timer for 10 minutes and press "Start/Stop" to begin preheating.

9. When the unit beeps to show that it is preheated, insert the air fry basket in the oven.

10. When the cooking time is completed, remove the air fry basket from the oven and serve hot.

Tangy Halibut

Servings: 2
Preparation Time: 15 minutes
Cooking Time: 12 minutes
Ingredients:
- 2 (5-ounce) halibut fillets
- 1 garlic clove, minced
- 1 teaspoon fresh rosemary, minced
- 1 tablespoon olive oil
- 1 tablespoon balsamic vinegar 1/8 teaspoon hot sauce
- 3 cups fresh baby greens

Directions:

1. In a large resealable bag, add all the ingredients except for greens.

2. Seal the bag and shale well to mix.

3. Refrigerate to marinate for at least 30 minutes.

4. Line a baking pan with a piece of foil.

5. Remove the fish fillets from bag and shake off the excess marinade.

6. Arrange the fish fillets into the prepared baking pan.

7. Arrange the pan over the wire rack.

8. Select "Bake" of Breville Smart Air Fryer Oven and adjust the temperature to 450 degrees F.

9. Set the timer for 12 minutes and press "Start/Stop" to begin preheating.

10. When the unit beeps to show that it is preheated, insert the wire rack in the oven.

11. When the cooking time is completed, remove the pan from the oven and serve alongside the greens.

Haddock with Tomatoes & Bell Peppers

Servings: 4
Preparation Time: 15 minutes
Cooking Time: 4 hours
Ingredients:
- 1 (15-ounce) can sugar-free diced tomatoes
- 1 green bell pepper, seeded and chopped
- 1 small onion, diced
- 1 garlic cloves, minced
- 1-pound haddock fillets
- 1 teaspoon dried herbs
- Salt and ground black pepper, as required 1/3 cup low-sodium chicken broth

Directions:

1. Lightly grease a Dutch oven that will fit in the Breville Smart Air Fryer Oven.

2. In the greased pot, place the tomatoes, bell pepper, onion and garlic and stir to combine.

3. Place the fish fillets on top of the tomato mixture and sprinkle with the herbs, salt and black pepper.

4. Place the broth on top evenly.

5. Arrange the Dutch oven over the wire rack.

6. Select "Slow Cooker" of Breville Smart Air Fryer Oven and set on "High".

7. Set the timer for 4 hours and press "Start/Stop" to begin cooking.

8. When the cooking time is completed, remove the Dutch oven from the oven.

9. Remove the lid and serve hot.

Green Beans with Carrots

Servings: 3
Preparation Time: 15 minutes
Cooking Time: 10 minutes
Ingredients:
- ½ pound green beans, trimmed
- ½ pound carrots, peeled and cut into sticks
- 1 tablespoon olive oil
- Salt and ground black pepper, as required

Directions:

1. In a bowl, add all the ingredients and toss to coat well.

2. Place the vegetables in the rotisserie basket and attach the lid.

3. Select "Air Fry" of Breville Smart Air Fryer Oven and adjust the temperature to 400 degrees F.

4. Arrange the vegetables into the greased air fry basket.

5. Set the timer for 10 minutes and press "Start/Stop" to begin preheating.

6. When the unit beeps to show that it is preheated, insert the air fry basket in the oven.

7. When the cooking time is completed, remove the air fry basket from the oven.

8. Serve hot.

Broccoli with Olives

Servings: 6

Preparation Time: 15 minutes

Cooking Time: 15 minutes

Ingredients:

* 1½ pounds broccoli head, stemmed and cut into 1-inch florets
* 2 tablespoons olive oil
* Salt and ground black pepper, as required
* 1/3 cup Kalamata olives, halved and pitted
* 2 teaspoons fresh lemon zest, grated

Directions:

1. In a pan of boiling water, add the broccoli and cook for about 3-4 minutes.

2. Drain the broccoli well.

3. In a bowl, place the broccoli, oil, salt, and black pepper and toss to coat well.

4. Arrange the broccoli into the greased air fry basket.

5. Select "Air Fry" of Breville Smart Air Fryer Oven and adjust the temperature to 355 degrees F.

6. Set the timer for 15 minutes and press "Start/Stop" to begin preheating.

7. When the unit beeps to show that it is preheated, insert the air fry basket in the oven.

8. After 8 minutes of cooking, toss the broccoli florets.

9. When the cooking time is completed, remove the air fry basket from the oven and transfer the broccoli into a large bowl.

10. Add the olives, lemon zest and cheese and stir to combine.

11. Serve immediately.

Peas with Mushrooms

Servings: 4

Preparation Time: 15 minutes

Cooking Time: 15 minutes

Ingredients:

* ½ cup soy sauce
* 4 tablespoons maple syrup
* 4 tablespoons balsamic vinegar
* 4 garlic cloves, chopped finely
* 2 teaspoons Chinese five-spice powder ½ teaspoon ground ginger
* 16 ounces Cremini mushrooms, halved ½ cup frozen peas

Directions:

1. In a bowl, add the soy sauce, maple syrup, vinegar, garlic, five-spice powder, and ground ginger and mix well.

2. Place the mushroom into the prepared baking dish in a single layer.

3. Select "Air Fry" of Breville Smart Air Fryer Oven and adjust the temperature to 350 degrees F.

4. Set the timer for 15 minutes and press "Start/Stop" to begin preheating.

5. When the unit beeps to show that it is preheated, arrange the baking dish over the wire rack.

6. After 8 minutes of cooking, add the peas and vinegar mixture into the baking dish and stir to combine.

7. When the cooking time is completed, remove the baking dish from the oven and transfer the vegetable mixture onto serving plates.

8. Serve hot.

Broccoli with Sweet Potatoes

Servings: 4

Preparation Time: 15 minutes

Cooking Time: 20 minutes

Ingredients:

* 2 medium sweet potatoes, peeled and cut into 1-inch cubes
* 1 head broccoli, cut into 1-inch florets
* 2 tablespoons vegetable oil
* Salt and ground black pepper, as required

Directions:

1. In a large bowl, add all the ingredients and toss to coat well.

2. Arrange the vegetables into the greased air fry basket.

3. Select "Roast" of Breville Smart Air Fryer Oven and adjust the temperature to 415 degrees F.

4. Set the timer for 20 minutes and press "Start/Stop" to begin preheating.

5. When the unit beeps to show that it is preheated, insert the air fry basket in the oven.

6. When the cooking time is completed, remove the air fry basket from the oven and transfer the vegetable mixture onto serving plates.

7. Serve hot.

Tofu with Peanut Butter Sauce

Servings: 3

Preparation Time: 20 minutes

Cooking Time: 15 minutes

Ingredients:

For Tofu:

- 2 tablespoons fresh lime juice
- 2 tablespoons soy sauce
- 1 tablespoon maple syrup
- 1 teaspoon Sriracha sauce
- 2 teaspoons fresh ginger, peeled
- 2 garlic cloves, peeled
- 1 (14-ounces) block tofu, pressed and cut into strips

For Sauce:

- 1 (2-inch) piece fresh ginger, peeled
- 2 garlic cloves, peeled
- ½ cup creamy peanut butter
- 1 tablespoon soy sauce
- 1 tablespoon fresh lime juice
- 1-2 teaspoons Sriracha sauce
- 6 tablespoons water

For Serving:

- 5 cups fresh baby spinach

Directions:

1. For tofu: in a food processor, put all the ingredients except tofu and pulse until smooth.

2. In a bowl, mix together the marinade and tofu.

3. Set aside to marinate for about 20-30 minutes.

4. Meanwhile, soak 6 bamboo skewers into the water for about 30 minutes.

5. With a cutter, cut each skewer in half.

6. Thread one tofu strip onto each little bamboo stick.

7. Arrange tofu skewers into the greased air fry basket in a single layer.

8. Select "Air Fry" of Breville Smart Air Fryer Oven and adjust the temperature to 370 degrees F.

9. Set the timer for 15 minutes and press "Start/Stop" to begin preheating.

10. When the unit beeps to show that it is preheated, insert the air fry basket in the oven.

11. For the sauce: add all the ingredients in a food processor and pulse until smooth.

12. When the cooking time is completed, remove the air fry basket from the oven and transfer the tofu cubes onto serving plates.

13. Top with the sauce and serve alongside the spinach

Stuffed Eggplants

Servings: 4

Preparation Time: 20 minutes

Cooking Time: 11 minutes

Ingredients:

- 4 small eggplants, halved lengthwise
- 1 teaspoon fresh lime juice
- 1 teaspoon vegetable oil
- 1 small onion, chopped
- ¼ teaspoon garlic, chopped
- ½ of small tomato, chopped
- Salt and ground black pepper, as required
- 1 tablespoon cottage cheese, chopped
- ¼ of green bell pepper, seeded and chopped
- 1 tablespoon tomato paste
- 1 tablespoon fresh cilantro, chopped

Directions:

1. Carefully cut a slice from one side of each eggplant lengthwise.

2. With a small spoon, scoop out the flesh from each eggplant, leaving a thick shell.

3. Transfer the eggplant flesh into a bowl.

4. Drizzle the eggplants with lime juice evenly.

5. Arrange the hollowed eggplants into the greased air fry basket.

6. Select "Air Fry" of Breville Smart Air Fryer Oven and adjust the temperature to 320 degrees F.

7. Set the timer for 3 minutes and press "Start/Stop" to begin preheating.

8. When the unit beeps to show that it is preheated, insert the air fry basket in the oven.

9. Meanwhile, in a skillet, heat the oil over medium heat and sauté the onion and garlic for about 2 minutes.

10. Add the eggplant flesh, tomato, salt, and black pepper and sauté for about 2 minutes.

11. Stir in the cheese, bell pepper, tomato paste, and cilantro and cook for about 1 minute.

12. Remove the pan of the veggie mixture from heat.

13. When the cooking time is completed, remove the air fry basket from the oven and arrange the cooked eggplants onto a plate.

14. Stuff each eggplant with the veggie mixture.

15. Close each with its cut part.

16. Again arrange the eggplants shells into the greased air fry basket and insert into the oven.

17. Select "Air Fry" of Breville Smart Air Fryer Oven and adjust the temperature to 320 degrees F.

18. Set the timer for 8 minutes and press "Start/Stop" to begin cooking.

19. When the cooking time is completed, remove the air fry basket from the oven and arrange the cooked eggplants onto serving plates.

20. Serve hot.

Carrot with Zucchini

Servings: 6

Preparation Time: 15 minutes

Cooking Time: 35 minutes

Ingredients:

- 6 teaspoons coconut oil, melted and divided
- ½ pound carrots, peeled and sliced
- 2 pounds zucchinis, sliced
- 1 tablespoon fresh basil, chopped
- Salt and ground black pepper, as required

Directions:

1. In a bowl, mix together 2 teaspoons of coconut oil and carrots.

2. Place the carrots into the air fry basket.

3. Select "Air Fry" of Breville Smart Air Fryer Oven and adjust the temperature to 400 degrees F.

4. Set the timer for 35 minutes and press "Start/Stop" to begin preheating.

5. When the unit beeps to show that it is preheated, insert the air fry basket in the oven.

6. Meanwhile, in a large bowl, mix together the remaining coconut oil, zucchini, basil, salt and black pepper.

7. After 5 minutes of cooking, place the zucchini mixture into the basket with carrots.

8. Toss the vegetable mixture 2-3 times during the coking.

9. When the cooking time is completed, remove the air fry basket from the oven and transfer the vegetable mixture onto serving plates.

10. Serve hot.

Parmesan Mixed Veggies

Servings: 5

Preparation Time: 15 minutes

Cooking Time: 18 minutes

Ingredients:

- 1 tablespoon olive oil
- 1 tablespoon garlic, minced
- 1 cup cauliflower florets
- 1 cup broccoli florets
- 1 cup zucchini, sliced
- ½ cup yellow squash, sliced
- ½ cup fresh mushrooms, sliced
- 1 small onion, sliced
- ¼ cup balsamic vinegar
- 1 teaspoon red pepper flakes
- Salt and ground black pepper, as required
- ¼ cup low-fat Parmesan cheese, grated

Directions:

1. In a large bowl, add all the ingredients except for cheese and toss to coat well.

2. Arrange the vegetables into the greased air fry basket.

3. Select "Air Fry" of Breville Smart Air Fryer Oven and adjust the temperature to 400 degrees F.

4. Set the timer for 18 minutes and press "Start/Stop" to begin preheating.

5. When the unit beeps to show that it is preheated, insert the roasting pan in the oven.

6. After 8 minutes of cooking, flip the vegetables.

7. After 16 minutes of cooking, sprinkle the vegetables with cheese evenly.

8. When the cooking time is completed, remove the roasting pan from the oven and transfer the vegetable mixture onto serving plates.

9. Serve hot.

Stuffed Pumpkin

Servings: 5

Preparation Time: 15 minutes

Cooking Time: 30 minutes

Ingredients:

- 1 sweet potato, peeled and chopped
- 1 parsnip, peeled and chopped
- 1 carrot, peeled and chopped
- ½ cup fresh peas, shelled
- 1 onion, chopped
- 2 garlic cloves, minced
- 1 egg, beaten
- 2 teaspoons mixed dried herbs
- Salt and ground black pepper, as required ½ of butternut pumpkin, seeded

Directions:

1. In a large bowl, mix well vegetables, garlic, egg, herbs, salt, and black pepper.

2. Stuff the pumpkin half with vegetable mixture.

3. Arrange pumpkin half into the greased air fry basket.

4. Select "Air Fry" of Breville Smart Air Fryer Oven and adjust the temperature to 355 degrees F.

5. Set the timer for 30 minutes and press "Start/Stop" to begin preheating.

6. When the unit beeps to show that it is preheated, insert the air fry basket in the oven.

7. When the cooking time is completed, remove the air fry basket from the oven and transfer the pumpkin onto a serving platter.

8. Set aside to cool slightly.

9. Serve warm.

Fueling Hacks Recipes

Yogurt Cookie Dough

Servings: 1

Preparation Time: 5 minutes

Ingredients:

- 1 sachet Lean and Green Essential Chocolate Chip Cookie
- 1 (5.3-ounce) container low-fat plain Greek yogurt

Directions:

1. In a bowl add Chocolate Chip Cookie and yogurt and mix until well combined.
2. Refrigerate to chill before serving.

Caramel Crunch Parfait

Servings: 1

Preparation Time: 10 minutes

Ingredients:

- 6 ounces low-fat plain Greek yogurt ½ packet stevia
- ¼ teaspoon vanilla extract
- 2 tablespoons whipped topping
- 1 sachet Lean and Green Puffed Sweet & Salty Snacks, crushed
- 1 tablespoon sugar-free caramel syrup

Directions:

1. In a bowl, mix together the yogurt, stevia and vanilla extract.
2. Top with whipped topping Puffed Snack sachet.
3. Drizzle with caramel syrup and serve.

French Toast Sticks

Servings: 3

Preparation Time: 15 minutes

Cooking Time: 4 minutes

Ingredients:

- 2 sachets Lean and Green Essential Cinnamon Crunchy Oat Cereal
- 6 tablespoons egg liquid substitute
- 2 tablespoons low-fat cream cheese, softened Olive oil cooking spray

Directions:

1. In a food processor, add the cereal sachets and pulse until fine breadcrumbs like consistency is achieved.
2. Add the egg liquid substitute and cream cheese and pulse until a dough form.
3. Divide the dough into 6 portions and shape each into a breadstick.
4. Heat a lightly greased skillet over medium-high heat and cook the French toast sticks for about 2 minutes per side or until golden brown.
5. Serve warm.

Fudge Balls

Servings: 2

Preparation Time: 10 minutes

Ingredients:

- 1 sachet Medifast chocolate pudding
- 1 sachet Medifast chocolate shake
- 4 tablespoons peanut butter powder
- ¼ cup unsweetened almond milk
- 2 tablespoons water

Directions:

1. In a small bowl, add all the ingredients and mix until well combined.
2. Make 8 small equal-sized balls from the mixture.
3. Arrange the balls onto a parchment paper-lined baking sheet and refrigerate until set before serving.

Coconut Smoothie

Servings: 1

Preparation Time: 5 minutes

Ingredients:

1 sachet Lean and Green Essential Creamy Vanilla Shake

6 ounces unsweetened almond milk

6 ounces diet ginger ale

2 tablespoons unsweetened coconut, shredded ¼ teaspoon rum extract

½ cup ice

Directions:

1. In a small blender, place all ingredients and pulse until smooth.

2. Transfer the smoothie into a serving glass and serve immediately.

Vanilla Shake

Servings: 1

Preparation Time: 5 minutes

Ingredients:

- ½ packet Lean and Green Vanilla Shake Fueling
- ½ packet Lean and Green Gingerbread Fueling
- ½ cup unsweetened almond milk
- ½ cup water
- 8 ice cubes

Directions:

1. In a small blender, place all ingredients and pulse until smooth.

2. Transfer the shake into a serving glass and serve immediately.

Tiramisu Shake

Servings: 1

Preparation Time: 5 minutes

Ingredients:

- 1 packet Medifast cappuccino mix
- 1 tablespoon sugar-free chocolate syrup
- ½ cup water
- ½ cup ice, crushed

Directions:

1. In a small blender, add all the ingredients and pulse until smooth and creamy.

2. Transfer the shake into a serving glass and serve immediately.

Shamrock Shake

Servings: 1

Preparation Time: 5 minutes

Ingredients:

- 1 packet Medifast Vanilla Shake
- 6 ounces unsweetened almond milk
- ¼ teaspoon peppermint extract
- 1-2 drops green food coloring
- 1 cup ice cubes

Directions:

1. In a small blender, place all ingredients and pulse until smooth.

2. Transfer the shake into a serving glass and serve immediately.

Berry Mojito

Servings: 2

Preparation Time: 10 minutes

Ingredients:

- 2 tablespoons fresh lime juice
- 6 fresh mint leaves
- 1 packet Medifast Mixed Berry Flavor Infuser
- 16 ounces seltzer water
- Ice cubes, as required

Directions:

1. In the bottom of 2 cocktail glasses, divide the lime juice and mint leaves.

2. With the bottom end of a spoon, gently muddle the mint leaves.

3. Now, divide the Berry Infuser and seltzer water into each glass and stir to combine.

4. Place ice cubes in each glass and serve.

Chocolate Shake

Servings: 1

Preparation Time: 10 minutes

Ingredients:

1 packet Medifast cappuccino mix

½ cup water

1 tablespoon sugar-free chocolate syrup ½ cup ice, crushed

Directions:

1. In a small blender, place all ingredients and pulse until smooth.

2. Transfer the shake into a serving glass and serve immediately.

Peanut Butter Cookies

Servings: 4

Preparation Time: 10 minutes

Cooking Time: 12 minutes

Ingredients:

- 4 sachets Lean and Green Essential Silky Peanut Butter Shake ¼ teaspoon baking powder
- ¼ cup unsweetened almond milk
- 1 tablespoon margarine, softened
- ¼ teaspoon vanilla extract

- 1/8 teaspoon sea salt

Directions:

1. Preheat your oven to 350 degrees F. Line a cookie sheet with parchment paper.

2. In a bowl, add the Peanut Butter Shake and baking powder and mix well.

3. Add the almond milk, margarine and vanilla extract and mix until well blended.

4. With a spoon, place 8 cookies onto the prepared cookie sheet in a single layer and with a fork, press each ball slightly.

5. Sprinkle each cookie with salt.

6. Bake for approximately 10-12 minutes.

7. Remove from the oven and place the cookie sheet onto a wire rack to cool for about 5 minutes.

8. Now, invert the cookies onto the wire rack to cool before serving.

Peanut Butter Bites

Servings: 1

Preparation Time: 10 minutes

Cooking Time: 1 minute

Ingredients:

- 2 tablespoons peanut butter powder
- 1 tablespoon water
- 1 sachet Lean and Green Essential Creamy Double Peanut Butter Crisp Bar

Directions:

1. In a bowl, add the peanut butter powder and water and mix until a smooth paste is formed.

2. In a microwave-safe plate, place the Crisp Bar and microwave for about 15 seconds or until soft.

3. Add the warm bar pieces into the bowl of water mixture and mix until a dough forms.

4. Make small 4 equal-sized balls from the dough and arrange onto a parchment paper-lined plate.

5. Refrigerate until set before serving.

Yogurt Cereal Bark

Servings: 2

Preparation Time: 10 minutes

Ingredients:

- 12 ounces low-fat plain Greek yogurt
- 1-2 packets zer0-calorie sugar substitute

- 1 sachet Lean and Green Essential Red Berry Crunch O's Cereal

Directions:

1. Line an 8x8-inch baking dish with a piece of foil.

2. In a bowl, add yogurt and sugar substitute and mix well.

3. Place the yogurt mixture into the prepared baking dish and spread in an even layer.

4. Sprinkle the Cereal sachet on top evenly.

5. Freeze overnight or until bark is hard.

6. With a sharp knife, cut the bark into small pieces and serve.

Sweet Potato & Cheese Muffins

Servings: 12

Preparation Time: 10 minutes

Cooking Time: 31 minutes

Ingredients:

- 4 sachets Lean and Green Honey Sweet Potatoes
- 1 cup unsweetened almond milk
- 4 eggs
- 2/3 cups part-skim ricotta cheese
- 1 ounce goat cheese, crumbled
- ¼ C. yellow onion, chopped
- 1 tablespoon fresh rosemary, chopped 1/8 teaspoon ground nutmeg

Directions:

1. Preheat your oven to 350 degrees F.

2. Lightly grease a 12 cups standard-sized muffin tin.

3. In a large microwave-safe bowl, add the Honey Sweet Potatoes sachets and almond milk and mix well.

4. Microwave on High for about 1½ minutes.

5. Remove from the microwave and stir the mixture well.

6. Set aside to cool.

7. After cooling, add the remaining ingredients and mix until well blended.

8. Place the mixture into the prepared muffin cups evenly.

9. Bake for approximately 25-30 minutes or until a toothpick inserted in the center comes out clean.

10. Remove the muffin tin from oven and place onto a wire rack to cool for about 10 minutes.

11. Carefully invert the muffins onto the wire rack to cool completely before serving.

Chocolate Coconut Pie

Servings: 2

Preparation Time: 10 minutes

Cooking Time: 20 seconds

Ingredients:

- 1 sachet Lean and Green Drizzled Chocolate Fudge Crisp Bar Olive oil cooking spray
- 2 tablespoons whipped topping
- 1 sachet Lean and Green Essential Chocolate Fudge Pudding ½ cup unsweetened coconut milk
- 1 tablespoon unsweetened coconut, shredded

Directions:

1. In a microwave-safe bowl, add the Chocolate bar and microwave on High for about 15-20 seconds.

2. Place the melted bar into a lightly greased ramekin and wit the back of a spoon, press it slightly.

3. In a bowl, add the Fudge pudding and milk and mix well.

4. Place the pudding mixture over the bar in ramekin and refrigerate for about 30 minutes.

5. Top with whipped topping and coconut and serve.

Chocolate Berry Parfait

Servings: 2

Preparation Time: 10 minutes

Ingredients:

- 1 sachet Chocolate Cherry Ganache Bar
- 1½ cups low-fat plain Greek yogurt
- ¼ cup strawberry-flavored light cream cheese, softened
- 1 tablespoon unsweetened cocoa powder
- 1-2 packets zero-calorie sugar substitute
- 2/3 ounce almonds, sliced

Directions:

1. In a blender, add all ingredients and pulse until desired consistency is achieved.

2. Serve immediately.

Chia Seed Pudding

Servings: 1

Preparation Time: 10 minutes

Cooking Time: 11 minutes

Ingredients:

- 2 sachets Lean and Green Chia Bliss Smoothie
- 1 cup unsweetened almond milk ¼ cup chia seeds

Directions:

1. In a serving bowl, add all the ingredients and mix until well blended.

2. Refrigerate overnight before serving.

Caramel Macchiato Frappe

Servings: 1

Preparation Time: 10 minutes

Ingredients:

- 8 ounces unsweetened cashew milk
- 1 sachet Lean and Green Essential Caramel Macchiato Shake
- ½ cup ice
- 2 tablespoons whipped topping
- 1 tablespoon sugar-free caramel syrup

Directions:

1. In a blender, add the Macchiato Shake sachet, cashew milk and ice and pulse until smooth.

2. Transfer the mixture into a glass and top with whipped topping.

3. Drizzle with caramel syrup and serve immediately.

Brownie Pudding

Servings: 1

Preparation Time: 5 minutes

Ingredients:

- 1 (5.3-ounce) container low-fat plain Greek yogurt
- 1 sachet Lean and Green Brownie Mix

Directions:

1. In a bowl, add yogurt and Brownie Mix sachet and mix well.

2. Refrigerate to chill before serving.

Vanilla Frappe

Servings: 1

Preparation Time: 5 minutes

Ingredients:

- 1 sachet Lean and Green Essential Vanilla Shake
- 8 ounces unsweetened almond milk
- ½ cup ice
- 1 tablespoon whipped topping

Directions:

1. In a blender, add the Vanilla Shake sachet, almond milk and ice and pulse until smooth.

2. Transfer the mixture into a glass and top with whipped topping.

3. Serve immediately.

Mint Cookies

Servings: 4

Preparation Time: 15 minutes

Cooking Time: 10 minutes

Ingredients:

- 2 sachet Lean and Green Essential Chocolate Mint Cookie Bars
- 2 sachet Lean and Green Essential Decadent Double Chocolate Brownie
- 2 tablespoons unsweetened almond milk
- 2 egg whites

Directions:

1. Preheat your oven to 350 degrees F.

2. Line a cookie sheet with parchment paper.

3. In a food processor, add the Chocolate Bars and pulse until crushed.

4. Transfer the crushed bar into a bowl with remaining ingredients and mix until well blended.

5. With a spoon, place 8 cookies onto the prepared cookie sheet in a single layer and with your fingers, press each ball slightly.

6. Bake for approximately 13-15 minutes.

7. Remove from the oven and place the cookie sheet onto a wire rack to cool for about 5 minutes.

8. Now, invert the cookies onto the wire rack to cool before serving.

Gingerbread Biscotti

Servings: 4

Preparation Time: 15 minutes

Cooking Time: 45 minutes

Ingredients:

- 1 sachet Lean and Green Essential Spiced Gingerbread ¼ teaspoon baking powder
- 2 tablespoons sugar-free maple syrup
- 2 egg whites

Directions:

1. Preheat your oven to 350 degrees F. Line a baking sheet with parchment paper.

2. In a bowl, mix together the gingerbread sachet and baking powder.

3. In the bowl, add the maple syrup and egg whites and mix until well blended.

4. With lightly greased hands, place the dough onto the prepared baking sheet.

5. With your hands, shape the dough into an 8-inch long log.

6. Bake for approximately 25-30 minutes or until the top is firm.

7. Remove the baking sheet from oven and set aside to cool for about 5-10 minutes.

8. Cut the log into 8 (1-inch thick) slices.

9. Arrange the biscotti slices onto the baking sheet in a single layer, cut side down.

10. Now, set the temperature of the oven to 325 degrees F and Bake for approximately 15 minutes.

11. Remove the baking sheet from oven and place the baking sheet onto a wire rack to cool for about 5 minutes.

12. Now, invert the biscotti sticks onto the wire rack to cool before serving.

Chocolate Frappe

Servings: 1

Preparation Time: 5 minutes

Ingredients:

- 1 sachet Lean and Green Essential Frosty Mint Chocolate Soft Serve Treat
- 4 ounces strong brewed coffee
- 4 ounces unsweetened almond milk
- 1½ tablespoons sugar-free chocolate syrup, divided ¼ teaspoon peppermint extract
- ½ cup ice

- 1 tablespoon whipped topping

Directions:

1. In a blender, add the Chocolate sachet, coffee, almond milk, 1 tablespoon of chocolate syrup, peppermint extract and ice and pulse until smooth.

2. Transfer the mixture into a glass and top with whipped topping.

3. Drizzle with remaining chocolate syrup and serve immediately.

Chocolate Crunch Cookies

Servings: 2

Preparation Time: 10 minutes

Cooking Time: 2 minutes 20 seconds

Ingredients:

- 1 sachet Lean and Green Brownie Mix
- 1 Peanut Butter Chocolate Crunch Bar
- 3 tablespoons water

Directions:

1. In a bowl, add the brownie mix and water and mix well. Set aside.

2. In a microwave-safe bowl, place the crunch bar and microwave on High for about 20 seconds or until it is slightly melted.

3. Add the crunch bar into the brownie mixture and mix until well combined.

4. Divide the mixture into 2 greased ramekins and microwave on High for about 2 minutes.

5. Remove from microwave and set aside to cool for about 5 minutes before serving.

Mozzarella Pizza Bites

Servings: 4

Preparation Time: 15 minutes

Cooking Time: 12 minutes

Ingredients:

- 4 packets Lean and Green Buttermilk Cheddar Herb Biscuit Olive oil cooking spray
- 3 plum tomatoes, sliced thinly
- 1 cup fresh basil leaves, julienned
- ½ cup unsweetened almond milk
- 2 teaspoons olive oil
- 4 ounces fresh mozzarella cheese, cut into small pieces
- 2 tablespoons balsamic vinegar

Directions:

1. Preheat your oven to 450 degrees F.

2. Lightly grease a 12 cups muffin tin.

3. In a bowl, add the Biscuit sachet, almond milk and oil and mix until well combined.

4. Place the Biscuit mixture into the prepared muffin cups evenly.

5. Place a mozzarella piece over Biscuit mixture, followed by the 1 tomato slice and basil pieces.

6. Bake for approximately 10-12 minutes or until cheese is bubbly.

7. Remove from the oven and set aside to cool slightly.

8. Serve warm with the drizzling of vinegar.

Gingersnap Cookies

Servings: 1

Preparation Time: 10 minutes

Cooking Time: 20 minutes

Ingredients:

- 1 sachet Lean and Green Essential Spiced Gingerbread
- 2 tablespoons cold water
- Olive oil cooking spray
- 2 tablespoons low-fat whipped cream cheese spread 1/8 teaspoon vanilla tract
- 3-5 drops liquid stevia

Directions:

1. Preheat your oven to 350 degrees F.

2. Lightly grease a cookie sheet.

3. In a bowl, add Spiced Gingerbread sachet and beat until smooth.

4. With a small spoon, place about 3 cookies onto the prepared cookie sheet in a single layer.

5. Bake for approximately 18-20 minutes or until golden brown.

6. Remove from the oven and place the cookie sheet onto a wire rack to cool for about 5 minutes.

7. Now, invert the cookies onto the wire rack to cool before serving.

8. Meanwhile, in a small bowl, place cream cheese, vanilla extract and stevia and beat until smooth.

9. Spread frosting over cookies and serve.

Blueberry Scones

Servings: 6
Preparation Time: 15 minutes
Cooking Time: 20 minutes
Ingredients:
* 4 sachets Lean and Green Blueberry Almond Hot Cereal ¼ cup ground flaxseed
* 1-2 packets zero-calorie sugar substitute ½ teaspoon baking powder
* 3 tablespoons frozen unsalted butter, cut into ½-inch pieces
* 3 tablespoons low-fat plain Greek yogurt
* ¼ teaspoon almond extract
* ¼ teaspoon ground cinnamon

Directions:
1. Preheat your oven to 400 degrees F. Line a baking sheet with parchment paper.
2. In a food processor, add the Hot Cereal sachet, flaxseed, sugar substitute and baking powder and pulse until well blended.
3. Add the butter and pulse until a coarse meal-like mixture is formed.
4. Add the yogurt and almond extract and pulse until just blended.
5. Place the dough onto the prepared baking sheet and shape into a 6-inch circle.
6. Sprinkle the top of the dough circle with cinnamon.
7. Bake for approximately 15-20 minutes or until top becomes golden brown.
8. Remove the baking sheet from oven and set aside to cool.
9. Cut the dough circle into 6 wedges and serve.

Marshmallow Cereal Treat

Servings: 1
Preparation Time: 5 minutes
Cooking Time: 1 minutes
Ingredients:
* 1 packet Medifast Meal Mixed Berry Cereal Crunch
* 2 tablespoons marshmallow dip

Directions:
1. In a small bowl, add the Cereal Crunch and marshmallow dip and mix well.

2. Place the mixture into a microwave-safe mini loaf pan and with the back of a spoon, press slightly.
3. Microwave for about 1 minute.
4. Remove from the microwave and set aside to cool completely before serving.

Sweet Potato Muffins

Servings: 1
Preparation Time: 10 minutes
Cooking Time: 15 minutes
Ingredients:
* 1 sachet Lean and Green Honey Sweet Potatoes
* ½ cup water
* 2 tablespoons eggbeaters
* ¼ teaspoon baking powder
* Pinch of ground cinnamon

Directions:
1. Preheat your oven to 350 degrees F.
2. Lightly grease 2 cups of a standard-sized muffin tin.
3. In a bowl, add all ingredient except for cinnamon and mix until well combined.
4. Place the mixture into the prepared muffin cups evenly and sorinkle with cinnamon.
5. Bake for approximately 15 minutes or until a toothpick inserted in the center comes out clean.
6. Remove the muffin tin from oven and place onto a wire rack to cool for about 10 minutes.
7. Carefully invert the muffins onto the wire rack to cool completely before serving.

French Toast Sticks

Servings: 3
Preparation Time: 15 minutes
Cooking Time: 4 minutes
Ingredients:
* 2 sachets Lean and Green Essential Cinnamon Crunchy Oat Cereal
* 6 tablespoons egg liquid substitute
* 2 tablespoons low-fat cream cheese, softened Olive oil cooking spray

Directions:
1. In a food processor, add the cereal sachets and pulse until fine breadcrumbs like consistency is achieved.

2. Add the egg liquid substitute and cream cheese and pulse until a dough forms.

3. Divide the dough into 6 portions and shape each into a breadstick.

4. Heat a lightly greased skillet over medium-high heat and cook the French toast sticks for about 2 minutes per side or until golden brown.

5. Serve warm.

Chocolate Donuts

Servings: 4

Preparation Time: 15 minutes

Cooking Time: 27 ½ minutes

Ingredients:

- 2 sachets Lean and Green Essential Decadent Double Brownie
- 2 sachets Lean and Green Essential Chocolate Chip Pancakes
- 6 tablespoons liquid egg substitute
- ¼ cup unsweetened almond milk
- ½ teaspoon vanilla extract
- ½ teaspoon baking powder

Directions:

1. Preheat your oven to 350 degrees F. Lightly grease 4 holes of a donut pan.

2. In a bowl, add all ingredients and mix until well blended.

3. Place the mixture into the prepared donut pan evenly.

4. Bake for approximately 12-15 minutes or until donuts are set completely.

5. Remove from the oven and set aside to cool slightly.

6. Serve warm.

Mini Chocolate Cakes

Servings: 2

Preparation Time: 10 minutes

Cooking Time: 18 minutes

Ingredients:

- 1 packet Medifast Chocolate Chip Pancakes
- 1 sachet Lean and Green Brownie Mix
- ¼ teaspoon baking powder
- ¼ cup water

Directions:

1. Preheat your oven to 350 degrees F. Grease 2 cups of a muffin tin.

2. In a bowl, add all the ingredients and mix until well combined.

3. Place the mixture into the prepared muffin cups evenly.

4. Bake for approximately 18 minutes or until a toothpick inserted in the center comes out clean.

5. Remove from the oven and place the muffin tin onto a wire rack to cool for about 10 minutes.

6. Carefully invert the muffins onto the wire rack to cool completely before serving.

Brownie Bites

Servings: 6

Preparation Time: 10 minutes

Ingredients:

- 3 tablespoons peanut butter powder
- 1 cup plus 3 tablespoons water, divided
- 6 sachets Lean and Green Double Chocolate Brownie Mix
- 1 cup water

Directions:

1. In a small bowl, add the peanut butter powder and 3 tablespoons of water and mix until well combined.

2. In another bowl, add Double Chocolate Brownie sachets and remaining water and mix until well combined.

3. In the bottom of 6 silicon molds, place the peanut butter powder mixture evenly and top with brownie mixture.

4. Freeze the molds until set completely.

5. Remove from the freezer and set aside for about 30-40 minutes before serving.

Chocolate Crepe

Servings: 1

Preparation Time: 10 minutes

Cooking Time: 4 minutes

Ingredients:

- 1 packet Medifast Chocolate Chip Pancakes
- ¼ cup water
- ¼ cup part-skim ricotta cheese
- ½ packet stevia powder
- 1/8 teaspoon vanilla extract
- 1 teaspoon sugar-free chocolate syrup

Directions:

1. In a bowl, add the pancake and water and mix well.

2. Heat a lightly greased skillet over medium heat.

3. Place the mixture and spread in a thin circle.

4. Cook for about 1-2 minutes per side or until golden brown.

5. Remove from the heat and place the crepe onto a plate.

6. In a small bowl, add the ricotta cheese, stevia and vanilla extract and mix until well combined.

7. Place the mixture inside the crepe.

8. Drizzle with chocolate syrup and serve.

Pumpkin Waffles

Servings: 2

Preparation Time: 10 minutes

Cooking Time: 8 minutes

Ingredients:

- 1 sachet Lean and Green Golden Pancake
- 1 tablespoon 100% canned pumpkin
- ¼ teaspoon pumpkin pie spice
- Pinch of ground cinnamon
- ¼ cup water
- 2 tablespoons sugar-free pancake syrup

Directions:

1. Preheat a mini waffle iron and then grease it.

2. In a bowl, add all ingredients except for pancake syrup and mix until well blended.

3. Place ½ of the mixture into the preheated waffle iron and cook for about 3-4 minutes or until golden brown.

4. Repeat with the remaining mixture.

5. Serve warm with the topping of pancake syrup.

Chocolate Cake Fries

Servings: 2

Preparation Time: 10 minutes

Cooking Time: 4 minutes

Ingredients:

- 2 sachets Lean and Green essential Golden Chocolate Chip Pancakes
- ¼ cup liquid egg substitute
- 2 teaspoons vegetable oil

Directions:

1. In a bowl, add Pancakes sachets and egg substitute and mix until well combined.

2. Place the mixture into a resealable plastic bag.

3. Cut off a small hole on tip of bag.

4. In a skillet, heat oil over medium heat.

5. In the skillet, pipe mixture in long, straight lines and vook forabout 2minutes per side.

6. Serve warm.

Yogurt Berry Donuts

Servings: 2

Preparation Time: 10 minutes

Cooking Time: 15 minutes

Ingredients:

- 2 sachets Lean and Green Yogurt Berry Blast Smoothie
- 2 tablespoons liquid egg substitute
- 1/3 cup unsweetened almond milk ½ teaspoon baking powder
- Olive oil cooking spray

Directions:

1. Preheat your oven to 350 degrees F.

2. Lightly grease 4 holes of a donut pan.

3. In a bowl, add the Smoothie sachets, milk, egg substitute and baking powder and mix well.

4. Divide the mixture into the prepared donut holes.

5. Bake for approximately 12-15 minutes.

6. Remove from the oven and set aside to cool slightly before serving.

Peanut Butter Cream Cupcakes

Servings: 4

Preparation Time: 15 minutes

Cooking Time: 15 minutes

Ingredients:

- 2 packets Medifast Original Pancakes
- 1 packet Medifast Original Style Eggs ½ teaspoon baking powder
- ½ cup unsweetened vanilla almond milk
- 4 teaspoons canola oil
- 2 tablespoons low-fat cream cheese
- 1 packet calorie-free sweetener
- 2 teaspoons powdered peanut butter ¼ teaspoon vanilla extract

- 1 packet Medifast Peanut Butter Soft Serve

Directions:

1. Preheat your oven to 350 degrees F.

2. Lightly grease 4 cups of standard-sized muffin tin.

3. In a bowl, add Original Pancakes sachet, Original Style Eggs sachet and baking powder and mix well.

4. Add almond milk and oil and mix until well combined.

5. Place the mixture into the prepared muffin cups evenly.

6. Bake for approximately 15 minutes or until a toothpick inserted in the center comes out clean.

7. Remove from the oven and place the muffin tin onto a wire rack to cool for about 10 minutes.

8. Carefully invert the muffins onto the wire rack to cool completely before filling.

9. With a paring knife, cut a large circle in the top of each cupcake, cutting down almost to the bottom.

10. Cut the bottom off of each of the cut-out cupcake pieces, leaving thin tops for each of the cupcakes.

11. Prepare Peanut Butter Soft Serve packet according to package's instructions.

12. Immediately fill each cupcake with Peanut Butter Soft Serve.

13. Place cupcake tops on top and freeze for about 1 hour.

14. For frosting: in a bowl, add cream cheese, sweetener, powdered peanut butter and vanilla extract and beat until well combined.

15. Spread frosting over cupcakes and serve.

Mini Biscuit Pizza

Servings: 1

Preparation Time: 10 minutes

Cooking Time: 14 minutes

Ingredients:

- 1 sachet Lean and Green Buttermilk Cheddar and Herb Biscuit
- 2 tablespoons water
- 1 tablespoon tomato sauce
- 1 tablespoon low-fat cheddar cheese, shredded

Directions:

1. Preheat your oven to 350 degrees F.

2. In a small bowl, add the biscuit and water and mix well.

3. Place the biscuit mixture onto a parchment paper and with a spoon, spread into a thin circle.

4. Bake for approximately 10 minutes.

5. Remove from the oven and spread the tomato sauce over the biscuit circle.

6. Sprinkle with cheddar cheese.

7. Bake for approximately 2-4 minutes or until cheese is melted.

8. Remove from the oven and set aside for about 3-5 minutes.

9. Serve warm.

Meringue Cups

Servings: 2

Preparation Time: 10 minutes

Cooking Time: 2¼ minutes

Ingredients:

- 2 Lean and Green Essential Zesty lemon Crisp Bars, crushed rouggly
- 1 ½ cups low-fat plain Greek yogurt
- 1 (o.3-ounce) box sugar-free lemon gelatin ½ teaspoon lime zest, grated

Directions:

1. Line 6 cups of a muffin tin with paper liners.

2. In a microwave-safe bowl, place Crisp Bar sachets and microwave for about 10-15 seconds.

3. Divide the crisp bar pieces into the prepared muffin cups evenly.

4. In another microwave-safe bowl, place yogurt and gelatin and microwave for about 2 minutes, stirring after every 40 seconds.

5. Remove from microwave and stir until smooth.

6. Place the yogurt mixture over crunch bar I each muffin cup.

7. Refrigerate for at least 1 hour before serving.

8. Garnish with lime zest and serving.

Snickerdoodles

Servings: 2

Preparation Time: 10 minutes

Cooking Time: 8 minutes

Ingredients:

- 2 packets Medifast French Vanilla Shake
- 1 packet Splenda with Fiber

- 1 teaspoon baking powder
- ¼ teaspoon ground cinnamon
- 1 teaspoon vanilla extract
- ¼ cup water

Directions:

1. Preheat your oven to 350 degrees F. Line a cookie sheet with parchment paper.

2. In a bowl, add the Vanilla Shake packet, Splenda, baking powder and cinnamon and mix well.

3. Add the vanilla extract and mix well.

4. Slowly, add the water and mix until a paste is formed.

5. With a spoon, place 4 cookies onto the prepared cookie sheet in a single layer and with your fingers, press ach ball slightly.

6. Bake for approximately 8 minutes.

7. Remove from oven and place the cookie sheet onto a wire rack to cool for about 5 minutes.

8. Now, invert the cookies onto the wire rack to cool before serving

Cinnamon Buns

Servings: 1

Preparation Time: 5 minutes

Cooking Time: 1 minute

Ingredients:

- 1 Medifast Pancake Mix
- 1 packet Splenda
- ¼ teaspoon ground cinnamon
- 1/8 teaspoon baking powder
- 2 tablespoons water
- ¼ teaspoon vanilla extract

Directions:

1. In a bowl, add all ingredients and mix until well combined.

2. Place the mixture into a greased microwave-safe bowl and sprinkle with extra cinnamon.

3. Microwave for about 50-60 seconds.

4. Serve warm.

Mocha Cake

Servings: 2

Preparation Time: 5 minutes

Cooking Time: 2 minutes

Ingredients:

- 1 packet Medifast Calorie Burn Cappuccino
- 1 packet Medifast Chocolate Chip Pancakes
- 1 packet Splenda
- 1 tablespoon egg beaters
- ¼ teaspoon baking powder
- ¼ cup water

Directions:

1. In a bowl, add all ingredients and stir until well blended.

2. Place the mixture into a greased 4-inch round microwave-safe dish and microwave on High for about 1¾-2 minutes.

3. Remove from the microwave and divide in 2 portions.

4. Serve warm.

Potato Bagels

Servings: 1

Preparation Time: 10 minutes

Cooking Time: 12 minutes

Ingredients:

- 2 egg whites
- 1 sachet Lean and Green Mashed Potatoes
- 1 teaspoon baking powder

Directions:

1. Preheat your oven to 350 degrees F.

2. Lightly grease 1 hole of a donut pan.

3. In a bowl, add the egg whites and beat until foamy.

4. Add the baking powder and mashed potatoes and beat until well blended.

5. Place the mixture into the prepare donut hole.

6. Bake for approximately 10-12 minutes or until done.

7. Serve warm.

Parmesan Chicken Bites

Servings: 3

Preparation Time: 15 minutes

Cooking Time: 30 minutes

Ingredients:

- 2 packets Medifast Parmesan Cheese Puffs, crushed finely
- 2 ounces boneless, skinless chicken breast, cubed

- 2 tablespoons low-fat Parmesan cheese, grated
- 2 tablespoons hot sauce

Directions:

1. Preheat your oven to 350 degrees F.

2. Line a baking sheet with parchment paper.

3. In a plastic Ziploc bag, place the crushed Parmesan puffs and Parmesan cheese and mix well.

4. In a bowl, add chicken cubes and hot sauce and toss to coat well.

5. Place the coated chicken cubes in bag with parmesan mixture.

6. Seal the bag and shake to coat well.

7. Arrange the coated chicken cubes onto the prepared baking sheet in a single layer.

8. Bake for approximately 25-30 minutes.

9. Serve warm.

Pizza Bread

Servings: 1

Preparation Time: 10 minutes

Cooking Time: 10 minutes

Ingredients:

- 1 packet Lean and Green Cream of Tomato Soup ¼ teaspoon baking powder
- Salt and ground black pepper, as required
- 2 tablespoons water
- ¼ cup low-fat cheddar cheese, shredded

Directions:

1. Preheat your oven to 425 degrees F. Grease a small baking sheet.

2. In a bowl, add the soup, baking powder, salt, black pepper and water and mix until well combined.

3. Place the mixture onto the prepared baking sheet and shape into a circle.

4. Bake for approximately 5 minutes.

5. Remove from the oven and with a spatula, flip the bread.

6. Top with the cheese and Bake for approximately 5 minutes more.

7. Serve warm.

Noodle Soup Chips

Servings: 1

Preparation Time: 15 minutes

Cooking Time: 18 minutes

Ingredients:

- 1 packet Lean and Green Chicken Noodle Soup
- 3 tablespoons water
- Olive oil cooking spray

Directions:

1. Preheat your oven to 375 degrees F.

2. In a small blender, add the soup sachet and pulse powdered finely.

3. In a small bowl, add the powdered soup and water and mix until dough ball forms.

4. Set aside for about 3-5 minutes.

5. Arrange the dough ball between 2 grease parchment papers and with your hands, flatten into a thinner circle.

6. Carefully remove the parchment paper from the top of the dough.

7. Carefully place the parchment paper with dough onto a baking sheet.

8. Bake for approximately 10 minutes.

9. Remove the baking sheet from the oven and with a sharp knife, cut into chips.

10. Arrange the chips onto the baking sheet in a single layer and Bake for approximately 6-8 minutes or until crispy.

11. Remove from the oven and set aside to cool before serving.

Chocolate Waffles

Servings: 2

Preparation Time: 10 minutes

Cooking Time: 8 minutes

Ingredients:

- 1 packet Medifast Chocolate Chip Pancakes ¼ teaspoon pumpkin pie spice
- 1 tablespoon 100% canned pumpkin
- ¼ cup water
- 2 teaspoons sugar-free pancake syrup

Directions:

1. Preheat a mini waffle iron and then grease it.

2. In a bowl, add all the ingredients except for pancake syrup and mix until well combined.

3. Place ½ of the mixture into preheated waffle iron and cook for about 3-4 minutes or until golden brown.

4. Repeat with the remaining mixture.

5. Serve warm with the topping of pancake syrup

Sriracha Popcorn

Servings: 1

Preparation Time: 5 minutes

Ingredients:

- 1 teaspoon unsalted butter, melted Teaspoon Sriracha
- Pinch of stevia powder
- 1 sachet Lean and Green Sharp Cheddar & Sour Cream Popcorn

Directions:

1. In a zip lock bag, place all ingredients.
2. Seal the bag and shake to coat well.
3. Serve immediately.

Snack Mix

Servings: 1

Preparation Time: 5 minutes

Ingredients:

- ½ sachet Lean and Green Puffed Sweet & salty Snacks
- ½ sachet Lean and Green Sharp Cheddar & Sour Cream popcorn
- 1 teaspoon Parmesan cheese, grated
- 1 teaspoon sugar-free caramel syrup

Directions:

1. In a zip lock bag, place all ingredients.
2. Seal the bag and shake to coat well.
3. Serve immediately.

Chicken Nuggets

Servings: 4

Preparation Time: 10 minutes

Cooking Time: 20 minutes

Ingredients:

- 1 egg
- 12 ounce boneless, skinless chicken breast, cubed Olive oil cooking spray
- 2 sachets Lean and Green Essential Honey Mustard & Onion Sticks, crushed finely

Directions:

1. Preheat your oven to 400 degrees F.

2. Line a rimmed baking sheet with a lightly greased piece of foil.

3. In a shallow bowl, crack the egg and beat well.

4. In another shallow bowl, place the crushed Onion Sticks.

5. Dip the chicken cubes in beaten egg and then coat with crushed sticks.

6. Arrange the coated chicken cubes onto the prepared baking sheet in a single layer and spray with cooking spray.

7. Bake for approximately 18-20 minutes, flipping once halfway through.

8. Serve warm.

Mac & Cheese Waffles

Servings: 2

Preparation Time: 10 minutes

Cooking Time: 9½ minutes

Ingredients:

- 2 packets Lean and Green Chipotle Mac & Cheese
- 6 tablespoons liquid egg whites
- 4 ounces cold water
- 2 tablespoons sugar-free maple syrup

Directions:

1. In a microwave-safe bowl, place Mac & Cheese packets and water and mix well.

2. Microwave on high for about 1-1½ minutes. Remove from microwave and stir well.

3. Set aside for about 1 minute.

4. Microwave on high for about 1 minute.

5. Remove from microwave and stir well. Set aside until cooled.

6. Add liquid egg whites and stir to combine.

7. Preheat a waffle iron and then grease it.

8. Place the mixture into the preheated waffle iron and cook for about 5-7 minutes or until golden brown.

9. Repeat with the remaining mixture.

10. Serve warm with the topping of maple syrup.

Oatmeal Waffles

Servings: 1

Preparation Time: 5 minutes

Cooking Time: 12minutes

Ingredients:

* 1 packet Medifast Oatmeal
* ½ teaspoon baking powder
* 2 tablespoons egg whites
* ½ teaspoon vanilla extract
* Pinch of Molly McButter
* Pinch of ground cinnamon
* ½ cup cold water
* 2 tablespoons sugar-free maple syrup

Directions:

1. Preheat a waffle iron and then grease it.

2. In a bowl, add all ingredients except for maple syrup and mix until well blended.

3. Place the mixture into the preheated waffle iron and cook for 6-7 minutes.

4. Carefully flip the waffle and cook for about 5 minutes or until golden brown.

5. Repeat with the remaining mixture.

6. Serve warm with the topping of maple syrup.

Taco Salad

Servings: 1

Preparation Time: 10 minutes

Ingredients:

* 5 ounces cooked extra-lean ground turkey
* 2 cups romaine lettuce, shredded
* ½ of medium orange bell pepper, seeded and chopped
* ¼ cup low-fat Mexican blend cheese, shredded
* 2 tablespoons pico de gallo
* 2 tablespoons lime vinaigrette
* 1 sachet Lean and Green Puffed Ranch Snack

Directions:

1. In a bowl, place turkey, lettuce, bell pepper, cheese and pico de gallo and mix well.

2. Drizzle with vinaigrette.

3. Top with Ranch Snack sachet and serve.

Shake Cake

Servings: 1

Preparation Time: 10 minutes

Cooking Time: 15 minutes

Ingredients:

* 1 packet Medifast Shake
* ¼ teaspoon baking powder
* 2 tablespoons water
* 2 tablespoons egg beaters

Directions:

1. Preheat your oven to 350 degrees F. Lightly grease a ramekin.

2. In a bowl, add all the ingredients and mix until well combined.

3. Place the mixture into the prepared ramekin.

4. Bake for approximately 15 minutes.

5. Remove the ramekin from oven and place onto a wire rack to cool for about 10 minutes.

6. Carefully invert the cake onto the wire rack to cool completely before serving.

Meal Plan 5 & 1

The 5&1 plan is the commonly prescribed Lean and Green diet plan because it is quite effective one. The 5 and 1 recommend you to take six small meals in a day. The meals should be divided in such a way that there should be "5 Fuelings" meals and "1 lean and green" meal in a day. For this, you can select any of the Lean and Green fuelings and add to the diet; when to consume the six meals is the dieter's personal choice. You can have 3 fuelings in the morning and afternoon then have a "Lean and green" meal in the evening and end the day with 2 fuelings. Remember, there should be 2-3 hours of the gap between two consecutive meals in a day. Since you will be using more of the fueling and less of the food on this plan, the weight loss is quickly achieved using this plan. And it is often suggested for the early stage of the Lean and Green weight loss program because it helps activates the fat burn.

Day 1:
Fueling Hacks:
Eggnog
Blueberry Scones
Chocolate Crepes
Chocolate Waffles
Mocha Cake
Lean & Green Meal:
Shrimp & Scallops with Veggies

Day 2:
Fueling Hacks:
Vanilla Shake
Chocolate Haystacks Potato Bagels
Mac & Cheese Chips
Snickerdoodles
Lean & Green Meal:
Turkey & Veggie Casserole

Day 3:
Fueling Hacks:
Coconut Smoothie
Chia Seed Pudding
Chocolate Donuts
Brownie Cookies
Tortilla Chips
Lean & Green Meal:
Steak & Veggie Salad

Day 4:
Fueling Hacks:
Chocolate Shake
Mint Cookies
French Toast Sticks
Pumpkin Waffles
Cheddar Pancakes
Lean & Green Meal:
Pork Stuffed Avocado

Day 5:
Fueling Hacks:
Vanilla Frappe
Parmesan Chicken Bites
Gingerbread Biscotti
Pizza Bread
Chia Seed Pudding
Lean & Green Meal:
Tofu with Kale

Day 6:
Fueling Hacks:
Shamrock Shake
Fudge Balls
Biscuit Pizza
Blueberry Muffins
Maple Pancakes
Lean & Green Meal:
Turkey & Spinach Stew

Day 7:
Fueling Hacks:
Peppermint Mocha
Soup Chips
Brownie Bites
Marshmallow Cereal Treat
Chicken Nuggets
Lean & Green Meal:
Chicken with Bell Peppers

Meal Plan 4 & 2 & 1

This is second plan is comparatively easier and simpler than the first plan. This approach recommends the use of 4 fuelings in a day along with 2 lean and green meals and 1 snack. The snack, in this case, should be healthy, and it should be free of carbs and sugars. Sure, this plan is relatively easy, but it does not guarantee quick results. It is overall healthy and can be used as a beginner's approach to starting with.

Day 1:
Fueling Hacks:
Chocolate Frappe
Peanut Butter Bites
Mocha Muffin
Mashed Potato Tortilla
Lean & Green Meals:
Veggie Stuffed Steak
Noodles Beef Taco Bowl
Snack:
4 ounces apple

Day 2:
Fueling Hacks:
Berry Mojito
Yogurt Cookie Dough
Sweet Potato Muffins
Sriracha Popcorn
Lean & Green Meals:
Chicken & Veggies Stir Fry
Tofu with Peas
Snack:
½ cup canned peaches (packed in water or natural juices)

Day 3:
Fueling Hacks:
Pumpkin Spice Latte
Chocolate Haystacks
Yogurt Berry Donuts
Buffalo Cauliflower Poppers
Lean & Green Meals:
Chicken & Veggie Quiche
Tempeh with Veggies
Snack:
4 ounces orange

Day 4:
Fueling Hacks:
Tiramisu Shake
Yogurt Cereal Bar
Brownie Peanut Butter Pudding
Taco Salad
Lean & Green Meals:
Salmon with Cauliflower Mash
Turkey Chili
Snack:
¾ cup low-fat plain yogurt

Day 5:
Fueling Hacks:
Caramel Macchiato Frappe
Cherry Mocha Popsicles
Smashed Potato Grill Cheese
Pumpkin Pie Trail Mix
Lean & Green Meals:
Stuffed Chicken Breast
Tofu with Broccoli
Snack:
½ cup fresh strawberries

Day 6:
Fueling Hacks:
Peppermint Mocha
Chocolate Berry Parfait
Blueberry Scones
Mozzarella Pizza Bites
Lean & Green Meals:
Shrimp with Zucchini
Turkey, Apple & Veggie Burgers
Snack:
3 celery stalks

Day 7:
Fueling Hacks:
Eggnog
Crunch Sandwich Cookies
Chocolate Cake Fries
Mac & Cheese Doritos
Lean & Green Meals:
Fish & Spinach Curry
Steak, Egg & Veggie Salad
Snack:
1 cup unsweetened cashew milk

Meal Plan 3 & 3

Once you have achieved the desired results, continue for 6 weeks with the 3&3 program so that your body gets used to maintaining the desired figure over time. For the weekly plan, feel free to do it your- self, another healthy habit so you don't feel obligated and can continue in freedom.

Conclusion

The Lean and Green diet is one of the most followed and effective diet programs.

Unlike other regimens, it is not designed for a specific health condition. It is designed according to the dietitian's needs to achieve the ideal weight and the healthy lifestyle you want.

The logic is that eating healthy recipes will make you feel full for a long time in contrast to foods that are high in carbohydrates and saturated fat. That's why it focuses on increasing the consumption of whole foods and reducing the use of fast commercial foods and other unhealthy foods.

The program has earned worldwide popularity for its ability to deliver sustainable results without complicating the meal program for people. It places very few restrictions on food and inspires people to choose a healthier version of their daily food without compromising on taste and nutrition.

Choosing the right diet or program had also become difficult as the industry flourished. Many diets claim to have specific health problems while helping a diet lose weight. The Lean and Green diet is the right solution!